Best Practices

for Serving

Young Adults

in School and

Public Libraries

Patrick Jones
and Joel Shoemaker

Introduction by
Mary Kay Chelton

Neal-Schuman Publishers, Inc.
New York　　　　　　　　　　　London

Published by Neal-Schuman Publishers, Inc.
100 Varick Street
New York, NY 10013

Library of Congress Cataloging-in-Publication Data

Jones, Patrick, 1961–
      Do it right! : best practices for serving young adults in school and public
libraries / Patrick Jones, Joel Shoemaker.
          p. cm. — (Teens @ the library series)
      Includes bibliographical references and index.
      ISBN 1–55570–394–1 (alk. paper)
      1. Young adults' libraries—United States. 2. Public libraries—Services
to teenagers—United States. 3. High school libraries—United States.
I. Shoemaker, Joel. II. Title. III. Series.

'18.5 J664 2001
62'6—dc21
                                                                    2001030718

(oo) All I'm askin'
(oo) Is for a little respect

Contents

Preface

Every time a teenager comes into a library is an opportunity to create a meaningful exchange between customer and librarian. How can we make the encounter positive? Will the customer leave feeling empowered and eager to return to use the library again? How do we encourage a positive experience for the librarian as well? Excellent, equitable customer service must be intentionally created, managed, maintained, evaluated, and rewarded. *Do It Right! Best Practices for Serving Young Adults in School and Public Libraries* discusses customer service principles as they apply to young adult library services and suggests specific strategies readers can use to provide their young adult library users with world-class customer service. Smart facility design, reliable equipment, and enlightened policies all enhance good service for young adults in libraries. Yet instinctively we know the most essential factor for good customer service is an intelligent, well-trained staff, sensitive to the special character of young adult service who truly enjoy working with teens.

Librarians serve young adults in both public and school libraries in an astonishing array of roles. We teach individuals, as well as both small and large groups. We promote literacy, teach traditional library skills, and teach information technology skills including practical, hands-on use of electronic communication, storage, and information appliances and equipment. School librarians juggle many roles. Students are always the primary focus but teachers and other adult colleagues also need a large portion of the librarian's time, resources, and energy. Public librarians are often generalists who strive to successfully provide customer service to young adults in addition to many other duties. *Do It Right! Best Practices for Serving Young Adults in School and Public Libraries* explores how all librarians can work to strengthen and improve the quality of service to young adults.

ORGANIZATION

The introduction is written by Mary K. Chelton, Associate Professor in the Graduate School of Library and Information Studies at Queens College, New York, and former President (1976-77) of the American Library Association's Young Adult Services Division (YASD), now called the Young Adult Library Services Association (YALSA). Chelton is also a prolific and respected writer, critic, and commentator on issues concerning teens and libraries. Her dissertation, "Adult-Adolescent Service Encounters: The Library Context" (1997), examined the relationships between teens and adult service providers in both public and school library contexts and identified stumbling blocks that interfere with the delivery of the highest quality service to this sizable and needy group of library customers. Her important work inspired us to write *Do It Right!*

We were intrigued by the fact that Chelton examined teens and the library staff who serve them in both public libraries and school libraries, as these two realms of librarianship are so often separated. In the sections of her dissertation focusing on public library staff and public library young adult patrons, we discovered much food for thought about ways teenaged customers are served in school libraries. Her exploration of the background about how and why young adults are often not treated with the kind of respect they need and deserve, both in society generally, and specifically in public and school libraries, illuminate the challenges we face as concerned professionals. It investigates solutions to improve the quality of service provided to teens in any library setting. Chelton has generously granted permission for us to quote extensively from her dissertation in this book. Whenever we excerpt passages from Chelton's dissertation, they will be formatted in a "box" with one of our discussions of or responses to her ideas immediately following.

We have divided our duties equally. Chapters 1 through 5, written by Joel Shoemaker, show how school library media specitlists' roles as advocates of literacy combined with their expertise in modern technologies for communication, storage, retrieval, and production of information perfectly position them for leadership in the delivery of the highest quality secondary education for today's teens. Chapter 1 introduces the provision of these best young adult customer service practices in the school library setting. Chapter 2 posits the ideal school library media center against the reality of the competing demands faced in the actual day-to-day delivery of service. Chapter 3 provides strategies for training support staff that play a vital role in delivering good customer service. Chapter 4 examines how new policies often affect service to students and the special circumstances surrounding the delivery of equitable service to special student populations. Chapter 5 provides means and strategies for evaluation of customer service, suggesting ways in which business may provide appropriate models for comparison or how, in other cases, business models may be less than ideal.

Chapters 6 through 11 are written by Patrick Jones. Chapter 6 explores aspects of developmental, social, and institutional concerns that impact the delivery of exemplary customer service to teens in public libraries. Chapter 7 describes how libraries can create "raving fans" out of teen customers and why it is so critically important that they do so. Chapter 8 emphasizes how the Internet, coupled with other changes in our society, requires new approaches in marketing. To meet the needs of today's teens, librarians can learn from retailers about these approaches to customer service quality and innovation. Chapters 9 and 10 cover strategies for improving customer service through reference service and at the information desk. These two chapters explain why the reference desk sometimes seems like ground zero and a battleground rather than the prime point for connecting young adults and libraries.

Chapter 10 provides an up-to-date, accessible, and informed overview of the magazines with special appeal to young adults, including descriptions for more than sixty magazines, as well as a discussion of other types of periodicals and serials popular among young adults. Chapter 11 shows how to create a customer service model for young adults via the research pathfinder that utilizes the power and flexibility of the World Wide Web to integrate important technology skills in both school and public libraries. Chapter 12 sums up the intent of improving YA customer service through the theme, "Kids Who Read, Succeed."

Do It Right! Best Practices for Serving Young Adults in School and Public Libraries shows ways customer service can become a focal point in your library. A positive customer service attitude among an active and caring staff trained in the appropriate skills to advocate for youth can do much to provide young adult library customers with the equitable library experience they need and deserve—library service that is characterized by personal and professional courtesy, tolerance, and respect.

Our experience as young adult librarians has shown us that our work is important. We want teenagers to learn, to grow, and to think in new and creative ways so that they can help solve the increasingly complex problems they face. We want them to be able and willing to make the best possible decisions. We believe reading, writing, reasoning, communicating, problem-solving, and other crucial skills can be developed and strengthened through excellent library services. *Do It Right! Best*

Practices for Serving Young Adults in School and Public Libraries offers practices to help you achieve this vision.

PATRICK JONES
JOEL SHOEMAKER

Acknowledgments

I would like to thank Elizabeth Martin, Leah Hiland, and Linda Waddle for setting my professional course, Mary Jo Langhorne and Jean Donham for waving the semaphores that brought me to Iowa City's media harbor, and my wife, Becky, for being my constant, guiding star.

—Joel Shoemaker

I would like to thank the staff, management, and administration of the Houston Public Library, in particular Alison Landers, Janine Golden, and Sheryl Berger. Hats off to the usual suspects as well: Erica Klein, Brent Chartier, Ken Rasak, and Betty Jones.

—Patrick Jones

Introduction: Contexts of Customer Service for Young Adults

Mary K. Chelton

"Adults tend to think of us as trouble . . .
they just want to get us off the streets and out of sight . . .
Nobody seems to care about helping us find a good path . . . ."
(McLaughlin, 2000: 17)

Whether librarians like it or not, they are in a "service" as well as an "information" profession these days, although the rhetoric of the field tends to downplay that aspect of the work. The two are not opposites, so it is wise not to assume that customer service for young adults in libraries is just great, and all that is lacking are new program ideas, information literacy lesson plans, or new technologies and all will be well. It is not accidental that the service guidelines from ALA that delineate the most proscribed unpleasant and unprofessional behavior toward users appears in *Directions for Young Adult Services* from the Young Adult Library Services Association (1993), or that the term "youth advocate" originated within this group of librarians. It is also interesting that the *Information Power* (American Association of School Librarians and Association for Educational Communications and Technology, 1998) standards for school library media services seem to assume a good service climate by the omission of attention to service in the school context, opting instead to reaffirm the teaching role of the school library media specialist through information literacy outcomes in students. Young adults are not a favored clientele in many libraries, so "customer service" to and for them can seem to take on a sort of urgency in public library discussions, or a sort of complacency in school library discussions.

Before discussing the specifics of customer service for young adults in any library context, it is perhaps wise to think about the larger social and developmental contexts within which these discussions are taking place. Since the second decade of the twentieth century, when compulsory schooling at the secondary level and the exclusion of child labor from the workplace began, American society has created structural social boundaries for adolescents. Both of these legislative initiatives were well intentioned on the surface to protect and educate youth, but they, in combination with other demographic changes, have had the unintended consequence of creating a structurally age-segregated society filled with intergenerational distrust. There are very few places where adolescents and adults naturally come together outside of school except in service encounters such as those which occur in shopping malls and libraries.

Another unintended consequence of socially constructed age segregation is the creation of an adolescent subculture, which, despite encompassing many other subcultures within itself, is held together and understood symbolically through music, dress, slang, humor, and style. These subculture symbols are often deliberately defiant of adult authority, not only to help distinguish adolescents from adults socially, but also to respond to the psychological individuation process going on within teenagers themselves. Entire industries now exist to reinforce the symbolic "glue" of the adolescent subculture; far fewer try to help them become integrated into the adult life they are excluded from but will soon be part of.

This structural and symbolic segregation from adults, in combination with the prevalence of guns and widely reported school violence, escalates the intergenerational distrust already present. The result is that adolescents are the bearers of a social "stigma" which categorizes them as "problems" even before they do anything. At a time during which identity is of paramount importance developmentally, American adolescents have to manage both a real personal and a "virtual" (that is, stigmatized) identity simultaneously in their social interactions. In service terms, this means that if they act and look like adults, they are taken seriously; if they act and look like adolescents, they are often viewed with suspicion, whether or not they deserve it.

PERVASIVE SOCIAL MYTHS

While adults have been lamenting the excesses of adolescents at least since the time of Aristotle, there are some widely held myths about adolescence in American culture that augment rather than dispel adult distrust of the age group. These myths are important because they are so taken for granted that social policy and services can be easily organized around them, when they are, in fact, misconceptions. The first myth, which can be traced back to the psychologist G. Stanley Hall, is that adolescence is a time of tumultuous upheaval, which must, at all costs, be kept under control. Since incidents involving teenagers are inevitably covered by the media from the perspective that the teenagers are a "problem," this myth is perpetuated daily, even though the opposite is true for the majority of adolescents. Library media frequently reproduces this myth in articles about managing "problem patrons," and in problem-centered listserv queries.

The second social myth is that adolescents are children, which is neither true biologically nor cognitively, but proves useful to ideologues who want to "protect" young people and to adult-managed organizations who merely want to control their behavior, lump them in with other age categories, or make no extra effort to serve them. Reproductive maturity and the ability to think and reason about phenomena not yet experienced are the hallmarks of adolescence, and neither are the attributes of "children." Ironically, when it comes to teenage pregnancy or dropping out of school, there are few adults who want to excuse the young people involved on the basis of their being "children" who did not know any better. Treating adolescents like children in service interactions is a foolproof way to make them avoid the place in the future, and teenagers will vote with their feet to go elsewhere.

The third myth is that adolescents are homogeneous, a possibly forgivable mistake because of the ways in which the all-look-the-same "dress code" of the subculture is misinterpreted by adults. This presumption, however, leads not only to incorrect global assumptions that all teenagers are irresponsible or up to no good, but also to a total misunderstanding of the incredible variability of the simultaneous "ages" that adolescents must juggle, and the implications of this variability for adult expectations and program development. Early adolescence is a period of development second only to early childhood in velocity. Many different changes occur simultaneously within the individual, but at different rates of growth—physical, social, emotional, psychological, cognitive, etc. In practical terms, this means that adult service providers, who frequently judge solely—and incorrectly—by appearance, cannot use this yardstick with this age group.

A teenager may look like all the other teenagers to an adult, because the young person is announcing that he or she is part of the subculture symbolically by the choice of costume, but that may say nothing about an individual's social or cognitive abilities. Neither can one make assumptions about young adults who look very mature or immature physically. As any science fiction convention-goer could relate, often the kids who are the brightest cognitively are the least developed physically or socially. Reading, writing, and socializing about science fiction seems to attract many adolescents like this. Libraries frequently set policies that presume homogeneity among their users that create problems with adolescents as a result.

A fourth myth is that adolescents and adults suffer from a "generation gap." While it is certainly true that there are generational differences in style, and some friction over the normal limit testing that adolescents put adults through, most young adults cherish their relationships with their parents and other adults who are special to them. Increasingly, though, time-bound adults have less and less time to spend with them, so the seemingly fleeting time spent by adults with adolescents in a service interaction is all the more precious for its scarcity.

DEVELOPMENTAL CHARACTERISTICS

There are two psychological characteristics common to adolescents, especially younger adolescents, as a result of the rapid physical and social changes occurring in their lives. People in this age group are hypersensitive to the opinions of others, or their perception of the opinions of others. David Elkind calls this the "imaginary audience." Even casual remarks or gestures which another adult would ignore, such as a department store clerk asking an overweight girl if she's looking for the maternity department, can infuriate or alarm young people who take these imagined slights quite personally.

Elkind calls the second psychological characteristic, which superficially seems to be the exact reverse of the imaginary audience, the "personal fable." The young person feels that he or she is alone in the universe and the only one who has ever had these feelings or experiences. This self-centeredness fades with experience, but while it is present the adolescent is truly oblivious to both the presence and the experiences of others. This is why stories in the first person with adolescent protagonists are so popular with many young adults, and also why the same kids are surprised to be put on notice that their behavior may be disturbing other people.

Figuring out who one is and hopes to be are major tasks of adolescence. Hartmut Mokros makes a powerful argument for the importance of communication in identity formation. Who we are socially is a product or by-product—a "gift"—of interactions with others. A person can unilaterally present himself or herself in a certain way, but only when others agree with that presentation and communicate that understanding back to the person is social identity secure. Identity formation is one of the prime developmental tasks of adolescence, so positive interactions with other people have a special importance at this stage of the lifespan.

CUSTOMER SERVICE DEFINED

"Customer service" is a combination of all the ways organizations give their users what they want and keep them happy. It is user-centered, not organization-centered behavior, communication, and attitudes. Most retail organizations understand that customer service is their prime method of retaining customers, because retention is what keeps them in business. It is simply too costly and difficult to attract brand new people continually. While giving good customer service does not mean doing *anything* customers want, it also does not mean blaming customers for the organization's inadequacies—sort of like, "If we don't have it, you don't want it"—nor is it turning unwanted customers into wanted ones through a variety of controlling routines. The latter technique is common among public sector institutions, like libraries, and young adults, without adults in tow to defend them, are often the victims of these routines. One size fits all behavioral rules are a good example of how libraries turn young adults into what facetiously might be called "60–year-old solitary intellectual mutes."

Discussions of customer service are always important but even more so now because the dynamics of service encounters are changing from interactions between persons within an ongoing relationship who are known to each other to interactions that are more impersonal with strangers, or made impersonal through the use of technology. While the reasons for these changes vary, the more instrumental and less relational encounter has become the norm for the young, in part because they have been both service provider as well as customer in such interactions because of the kind of jobs open to them while they are adolescents. The problem with this ubiquitous type of service encounter between strangers is that it is almost instantly dependent on first impressions, many of which can be stereotypical and unfair in terms of the real people interacting with each other without the time or the incentive to get to know each other. For a group such as adolescents who are already stigmatized, these encounters may be problematic because the young adults are too often perceived negatively by service providers. The adolescents, in turn, may be suspicious of service providers who attempt to have relationships with them, since this is outside their everyday experience of service. In fact, it may be that in today's social environment, some young adults may interpret such attempts as suspicious and possibly predatory.

A group of academics that has tried to measure service quality, which is a large component of "customer service," define it as the difference between expectations and perceptions of service. What makes this definition particularly useful is that both expectations and perceptions may be manipulated by the service organization. Many young adults expect adults in service situations to treat them badly because of pervasive unpleasant experiences in school offices, with the police, or in stores, restaurants, and movie theaters. Rather than reproducing these demeaning encounters, libraries can change YA expectations and perceptions. Kids are often kept waiting without explanations or distractions in service settings when a variety of simple techniques already exist to make the wait, or the perception of waiting, less annoying, such as a simple sign explaining why the person has to wait with an estimate of how long the wait will be. Just an accurate explanation of how long an interlibrary loan or a new materials purchase request will take can favorably alter expectations, assuming that these services are as routinely offered to adolescents and to adults on an equitable basis.

While perceptions can be managed and changed, it is important to understand that since bad experiences make people feel bad, they are remembered long after whatever was the excuse for the experience in the first place. Attention to emotions through body language, tone of voice, etc., on the part of service providers is absolutely vital with adolescents, especially because they are often confused and inarticulate and self-conscious about what they want. These are the ways in which one communicates that the other is valued and validated as a worthwhile person. A friendly service interaction is much more than an instrumental means to an end like retrieving a book or finishing a homework assignment. It is a gesture of care, something sorely needed by adolescents as they try to figure out who they are in an increasingly confusing and complex world.

REFERENCES

American Association of School Librarians and Association for Educational Communications and Technology. 1998. *Information Power: Guidelines for School Library Media Programs.* Chicago: American Library Association and Washington, DC: Association for Education Communications and Technology.

McLaughlin, Milbrey W. 2000. *Community Counts: How Youth Organizations Matter for Youth Development*. Washington, DC: Public Education Network.

Young Adult Library Services Association. 1993. *Directions for Library Service to Young Adults*. Second Edition. Chicago: American Library Association.

SOURCES

Chelton, Mary K. 1997. *Adult-Adolescent Service Encounters: The Library Context*. Ph.D. dissertation. New Brunswick, NJ: Rutgers University.

Chelton, Mary K. 2000. "Waiting Management in the School Library Media Center Service Environment," *Knowledge Quest* 28 (January/February): 46–47.

Dryfoos, Joy G. 1998. *Safe Passage: Making It Through Adolescence in a Risky Society—What Parents, Schools, and Communities Can Do*. New York: Oxford University Press.

Elkind, David. 1984. *All Grown Up & No Place to Go: Teenagers in Crisis*. Reading, MA: Addison-Wesley.

Goffman, Erving. 1963. *Stigma: Notes on the Management of Spoiled Identity*. New York: Simon & Schuster.

Gutek, Barbara A. 1995. *Dynamics of Service: Reflections on the Changing Nature of Customer/Provider Interactions*. San Francisco: Jossey-Bass.

Hebdige, Dick. 1983. *Subculture: The Meaning of Style*. London: Methuen.

Hernon, Peter, and Ellen Altman. 1998. *Assessing Service Quality: Satisfying the Expectations of Library Customers*. Chicago: American Library Association.

Hine, Thomas. 1999. *Rise and Fall of the American Teenager*. New York: Avon.

Kett, Joseph F. 1977. *Rites of Passage: Adolescence in America 1790 to the Present*. New York: Basic Books.

Lipsitz, Joan. 1975. *Growing Up Forgotten: A Review of Research and Programs Concerning Early Adolescence*. Durham, NC: Learning Institute of North Carolina.

Lipsky, Michael. 1980. *Street-Level Bureaucracy: Dilemmas of the Individual in Public Services*. New York: Russell Sage Foundation.

Luker, Kristin. 1996. *Dubious Conceptions: The Politics of Teenage Pregnancy*. Cambridge, MA: Harvard University Press.

McLaughlin, Milbrey W., Merita A. Irby, and Juliet Langman. 1994. *Urban Sanctuaries: Neighborhood Organizations in the Lives and Futures of Inner-City Youth*. San Francisco: Jossey-Bass.

Mokros, Hartmut B. 1996. "From Information and Behavior to Interaction and Identity." Pp. 1–24 in *Interaction and Identity: Information and Behavior Volume 5*, ed. Hartmut B. Mokros. New Brunswick, NJ: Transaction.

Parasuraman, A., L. L Berry,. and V. A. Zeithaml. 1990. "Guidelines for Conducting Service Quality Research," *Marketing Research* 2, no. 4: 34–44.

Schwartz, B. 1975. *Queuing and Waiting: Studies in the Social Organization of Access and Delay*. Chicago: University of Chicago Press.

Prelude:
The Moment of Truth Rap

Patrick Jones

Libraries have lots of rules. How about this one: the "golden rule." Treat others as you would want to be treated. Kind of an old concept for the new age, but it works. The primary problem with serving teenagers in libraries, however, is that adults and teens are not treated or served equitably in most libraries. While we don't have empirical evidence to back up this statement, there is plenty of anecdotal evidence from across the country to support this thesis. Teens are underserved, mistreated, and "coped with" rather than served. We can not expect to change the dynamic of customer service interactions without first reshaping the attitudes, paradigms, and contexts from which those interactions emerge. Let's start by framing the situation positively: teens are not a problem to be solved, but rather customers who bring us their informational, recreational, and educational problems. Our job is to assist them in solving their problems and to do so in such a way that they leave with "good feelings." That is YA library work in a nutshell: solving problems and providing good feelings. But remember, teens themselves are not problems. If library staff continues to see them as such, then nothing will change. Could one reason for this unequal treatment, this poor service, this neglect and disrespect, simply be because librarians forget what it was like to be 14?

As a prelude to thinking about the context of customer service, as a warm-up to developing ideas to improve this service, and as a starting point for adjusting our own attitudes, let's recall what it is like to be 14.

After each question, close your eyes and answer the question, not with words but with images, sounds, and textures. Let your senses work overtime. Turn off your brain, tune into your memories, and get in touch with that 14–year-old who once lived inside of you.

Remember where you lived when you were 14. Was it a house or an apartment?

9

What did it look like on the outside? Was it brick, wood, aluminum siding, or what? What color was it?

Can you remember the street address? Can you see those numbers and that street name?

What did the front yard look like? In the winter? In the summer? In the spring? In the fall?

Now, go into the house. How did you usually enter the house when you were growing up? Was there a porch? Did you enter through the front door, side door, or maybe a back door? What color was the door? Do you remember the sound it made opening and closing?

Walk into the house, shut the door, then look down. What did the floor look like?

Was it covered with carpet? If so, what color? Can you bend down and touch the floor?

As you look around from the entryway, can you recall how the house smelled?

Good, now let's go to the room that was your room. Did you have your own room? Or did you share a room with a brother or sister?

Let's go into that room that you called yours. Let's look around.

Was there paint on the walls or wallpaper? Was it light-colored or dark? What was the shape of the room? Were there any windows? Curtains? A shade? What furniture do you remember? Was there a dresser? Did you have a collection of makeup? Where did you keep it?

Go over to the bed. Lay down and look up at the ceiling. Was there a light fixture? What kind of pattern did it make on the ceiling? What color was the ceiling?

Now, let's look at the walls. Do you see posters? If so, of who? Frankie Avalon? The Beatles? Jon Bon Jovi? Bjork? Maybe an art print? Maybe a poster of horses or one of cats? What did the walls look like?

Are there shelves in the room? What were some of your favorite things on those shelves? Stuffed animals? Books? Trophies, awards, or photographs? Think about those things and what they meant to you.

Get up from the bed and put on some music. How would you have done that? Turn on a transistor radio? Put a record on a turntable? Insert a tape? Slide in a compact disc? Select a tune from the playlist on your computer? What was the single best song in the world you could have heard at age 14?

Can you hear it? The music, the beat, the vocals and lyrics? Listen—how does that music make you feel? Who or what does it make you think about?

Good. Let's find a mirror in your room or in the house. Where would it be?

Walk there and look into the mirror. Look at the 14–year-old version of yourself standing there.

Were you too tall? Too short? Too thin? Too fat? What did your hair look like? What did your skin look like? Were you happy with the way you looked?

Were you a happy person?

Let's look into those eyes now staring back at you. Let's look behind the eyes of that 14–year-old you. What do you see?

What were the emotions going on behind those eyes when you were 14?

Were you happy? Sad? Angry? Relaxed? Fearful? Confident? Feeling smart? Feeling stupid? Lonely? Loved? Did you feel all of these things intensely and daily? Let's hang on to those feelings for a while.

Let's get out of the house. Let's go to a library. Did you use a library when you were 14? If so, was it your school library or your public library? Go there now. How would you get there? Walk? Get a ride from your parents? Ride your bike? How close is it? What did it look like on the outside? Was it a big old Carnegie building with a formal flight of steps in front? Was it an open-classroom style media center in the center of the school?

Open the door, walk inside. What do you see? A counter with people behind it? A big, high-ceilinged room, dimly lit and quiet, with tables and chairs? Or perhaps a modern, fluorescent-lit suburban style room with displays and open spaces? Is there a card catalog? Are there computers?

Do you need some help? Look around to see who is available to assist you. What do they look like? Will you approach them to ask

*for help? Or will they approach you? Remember why you are in
the library today. What problem—needing a book, information for
a report, meeting friends, whatever—what problem needed to be
solved?*

*Good. Take a minute to remember that typical visit to that library.
Can you picture the scene? Were you alone or with friends? Where
were you sitting? Were you working quietly and diligently, or doing something else? What kind of mood were you in and why? Did
you regard the library staff as friendly and helpful or as the enemy, to be avoided if at all possible? Can you remember an interaction, a temporary relationship, with anyone there? Do you
remember any interaction with the librarian or staff?*
*If so, this is where we need to look for a moment of truth. Can you
remember an incident, a critical incident, from any visit to a library
when you were a teenager? Can you remember the scene? What
happened?*
*Now, if the incident you remember was a positive one, if the per-
son you encountered helped you, was friendly, was respectful and
made you feel good, then I want you to try to remember that feeling. Remember it and hang on to it. Pledge, put in writing, that
you will try your best to make sure that you—and everyone you
work with—provides the teens you encounter on a daily basis with
just such a positive memory. Pledge that each teen's moment of truth
will similarly result in good feelings and a solution to a problem.*

*But some of you might remember a different moment of truth. Some
of you might remember a person who was not respectful, not helpful. You might recall a person who left you with no good feelings
and maybe didn't even solve your problem. Did someone tell you
to get out of the adult area or might someone have questioned what
you were reading? Maybe someone yelled at you or just wasn't very
nice. If that was your critical incident, your moment of truth, then
hang on to that. Remember it and pledge, put in writing, that you
will try your best to make sure that you—and everyone you work
with—never, ever treats another teenager the way you were treated.*

This is our prelude and suggests the kinds of "connections" that can
help you provide quality customer service to teenagers in libraries. First,
remember that every encounter is a moment of truth and that any encounter may be the critical incident which shapes a person's attitudes

about libraries and librarians for years to come. Second, use this rap when serving customers to ensure that you and your library don't get a "bad rap" with teens:

- Remember—what it was like to be that 14-year-old
- Accept—that 14-year-olds act the way they do, as you did, just because
- Project—yourself into that 14-year-old customer in the library, and then
- Serve—that 14-year-old person as you were served or SHOULD have been served.

Chapter 1

Customer Service in the School Library Media Center

Joel Shoemaker

"The secret of education lies in respecting the pupil." *(Bradley, Daniels, and Jones, 1969: 242)*

Ralph Waldo Emerson

Soon after my arrival in Iowa in 1976 I encountered a teacher (let's call him Fred) at an evening's repast. Fred was nearing retirement. Talking with him about the fact that I was about to begin a new job teaching reading in a neighboring district, Fred advised, "The problem with schools today is that kids have no respect. There was a time when if you told a student to do something, he did it. There was a time when if a student was in trouble at school he was also in trouble at home. There was a time when kids showed respect for teachers, but that time is long gone. Schools today are going to hell."

That attitude just didn't sit right with me. I was young enough that I still identified more with teenagers than I did with him. I told him that I heard what he was saying—teens can be brash and abrasive and offensive, demanding and inconsiderate—who among us is not, sometimes? But I also told him that in my opinion respect must be mutual. One way to gain the respect of young people is to show them respect. Easy ways to do this include talking with them, listening to them, and being aware of their needs and wants. Get to know them as individuals, learn their names, watch the same TV shows and movies that they do and listen to their music. Remember what it was like to be their age. When you do these things, understanding may begin to come.

When one respects students, one strives to instill the desire to achieve that is central to teaching any subject to any student at any time. This begins to get at the "art" part of teaching, in which students willingly, even enthusiastically, give themselves up to the group endeavor or to the process, to learn from the experience they are about to encounter. It requires that the students be willing to take a certain amount of risk. They must give up some short-term autonomy or independence in order to learn from the work that is underway. They must agree to temporarily subvert their identity a bit so that the teacher can support, facilitate, coach, or teach the students into and through a learning experience. A golden-rule-like principle is at work here for both the teacher and the student: respect others as you wish to be respected. This has got to be as true when dealing with teenagers as it is for dealing with any other age group.

There is certainly evidence to suggest that our student population is changing. Changing demographics, however, must never become an excuse for poor teaching, an apology for low test scores, nor a euphemism for racism. It is simply a matter of fact that compared with students who were in our schools just a few years ago there are increases in the number and percentage of students who are:

- receiving free and reduced lunch (Dyke, 2000: 1A+)
- identified with learning disabilities
- enrolled in remedial, at-risk, and behavior disorder programs
- taught for at least part of the day in special education programs including resource programs
- reading below grade level according to standardized test scores
- taking Ritalin® and other mind- and mood-altering prescription drugs

Numerous accommodations are made by classroom teachers to meet the needs of these students. More associates continue to be hired to "shadow" and support individual students throughout all or part of their day in an effort to help them succeed. These and other factors have an impact on what we can teach and how we teach it.

Today's generation of teens is different than any previous generation in two important respects. First, the worldwide presence of AIDS means that their lives are at greater risk than ever before. Second, the global digital communications network makes it increasingly possible for a large portion of today's youth to plug into information in its broadest sense anywhere, anytime. It is ironic, isn't it, that as the youth population's reach exceeds anything previously imaginable, their errant, intimate touch may come back to kill them? The possibility of universal world-wide atomic destruction, still present as an international political cataclysm, has been trumped by the terrifyingly real possibility of personal self-destruction if they simply answer that most basic biological imperative of engaging in sex.

In the last generation or so, our libraries have by and large converted from analog card catalogs to digital computerized catalog systems. Circulation has similarly changed from a manual, hand-operated analog system to automated systems that offer possibilities for data gathering and manipulation that were unimagined in the not-so-distant past. Print materials, especially encyclopedias and other reference materials, have been converted to CD-ROM and online databases and indexes. The Internet itself has been transformed in only the last decade from a fairly esoteric medium of interest to relatively few people to—well, to everything that it is becoming today—another ubiquitous communication network for the middle class and more.

Those few fuzzy black-and-white network broadcast stations we had back in the fifties, sixties, and seventies have exploded into hundreds of narrowcasts beamed into our heads in living color; always on, always saying, "Look at me. Be like this. Buy that. Buy LOTS of that." Whether considering access to data, video, music, games, movies, or telecommunications, we are becoming one digitally linked world.

Information Power: Building Partnerships for Learning tells us that "Student achievement is the bottom line" (American Association of School Librarians and Association for Educational Communications and Technology, 1998). In today's world, young adults need both to master the old skills—reading, writing, arithmetic, working alone as well as with others, finding intrinsic and extrinsic rewards in life—and acquire new sets of skills for using new tools and new media for transforming themselves throughout their lives. They need to learn to make more and better decisions in their personal lives than any generation before them. They need time to be who they are now and time to grow up. That is, they will continue to be teenagers, experiencing the developmental processes that require them to be risk-taking, caring, inexperienced, challenging, energetic, undirected, inner-directed, insightful, frustrating, maddeningly talented—sometimes all in the same hour. They must become educated citizens of this new digital world. It seems clear to me that they need libraries and they need to know how to use them. As librarians we must strive to serve their needs by applying our best human and professional resources: knowledge, experience, understanding, courtesy, and time.

And the sum of these, as noted by America's foremost epigrammatist in this book's frontispiece, is r-e-s-p-e-c-t.

REFERENCES

American Association of School Librarians and Association for Educational Communications and Technology. 1998. *Information Power: Building Partnerships for Learning.* Chicago: American Library Association and Washington, DC: Association for Educational Communications and Technology.

Bradley, John P., Leo F. Daniels, and Thomas C. Jones, comps. 1969. *The International Dictionary of Thoughts.* Chicago: J. G. Ferguson Publishing Company.

Dyke, Jennifer. 2000. "Population Shift Forces Schools to Plan Ahead." *Iowa City Press-Citizen.* (March 18): 1A+

Chapter 2

Library Heaven

Joel Shoemaker

Have you ever been to library heaven? Sometimes I walk into my library and look around at all the activity going on and I just feel giddy. A warm feeling wells up from deep inside, a smile spreads across my face and out pops the thought, *"This* is library heaven!"

At that moment I am content. My library is exactly what I want it to be. The look of the place, the sounds and the activity going on are the fulfillment of all the years of hard work by my staff and myself and the entire educational community in which we work. What is it like? People fill the place. They are busy. Many are seated at tables, although some move from place to place. It is not particularly quiet. Students and adults in the room are engaged, working in all sorts of modes. Some work individually, perhaps reading and writing. Others are talking in small groups, and perhaps elsewhere in the facility one or two teachers are working with their entire class. People are reading books, newspapers, and magazines. They are clicking away at computer keyboards, printing, using other learning tools and the copy machine. In library heaven, the copy machine works.

Interactions between staff and customers are marked by mutual respect. The library media center is full, but staff performs their duties unobtrusively, efficiently, and correctly. They are friendly and approachable. The library staff works seamlessly with teachers and other building support staff in an efficient, congenial, and collegial atmosphere. It is evident that the staff is happy to be there. Although they are busy, they take as much time as is necessary to listen to customer requests and provide exactly the help that is needed. Not only is this assistance provided in a timely fashion, it is presented in such a way as to leave the customer empowered so that they will be able to work more independently the next time they come to the library. Customers know that when they have a problem or a question, the library media center staff will promptly act on their behalf in a way that is friendly, capable, accurate, and instructive. Customers know that they can depend on us to help them succeed. We will not let them fail. We will provide the help they need so that they can be successful.

Browsers comb the stacks. Kids are passing books back and forth to each other as they talk quietly in the paperback corner. Students come and go as needed, getting their passes signed by whichever staff member is closest. Arriving students often go to the computers and spend a few minutes using the catalog before going to the shelves to find their books. They help each other as they move back and forth from the computer catalog to the nearby stacks, searching out just the right book or other resource for the job at hand. Of course, since this is library heaven, every book they want is on the shelf and in good condition. In the unlikely event that all the available copies of a book are checked out, the student may place the book on reserve so that the next available copy is provided to them as soon as it is returned. If a requested title is not in our collection, interlibrary loan fills the need by the following day. Students use the library's computers to access the local public library's catalog and other online sources to obtain the information they need and want. Gazing around the facility one can see students using the Internet (which is never down and which is available at a sufficient number of workstations) to write papers, create original multimedia projects, and use productivity software to synthesize what they have found and analyze what they have learned. They create products that they save into portfolios that will later be used for assessment of specific, locally developed and community supported learning objectives. They use the computer network to store and back up their work. When they are ready to present their work to their class they may do so from any station, anytime, anyplace in an efficient, fast, and flexible "diskless" networked environment.

Library staff, teachers, associates, and students work together and help each other in the production room. They are laminating, getting supplies, and creating instructional and presentation materials such as posters and spiral-bound books. Someone is using the phone. The video cameras are being wheeled out on tripods for use in a classroom and will be returned promptly after class for the next customer. Someone is editing videotape nearby.

At the circulation desk, materials are quickly checked out to departing customers by well-trained, friendly, and competent student assistants who are careful to meet and greet each student as they arrive and again when they leave. No students have overdue materials and there is no theft in library heaven. A parent volunteer is sorting and then reshelving books. Sometimes worn books need to be repaired, and that task is handled expeditiously and expertly by trained support staff. Normal wear and tear requires occasional replacement of worn copies of the most popular titles, but there is little loss of books and deliberate vandalism is practically unknown, so most of the book budget is available for the purchase of the best new books available.

Teachers come and go throughout the day. A social studies teacher stops in to return a stack of new books she has previewed. Another consults with the library media specialist about an upcoming unit of study for which she has scheduled time for her classes to use the library to prepare a research-based project. Others use their prep periods to pick up or return materials, to learn to use and then check out various pieces of audiovisual equipment, or to sit, relax a bit, and read the paper or magazines. The rooms are well illuminated and are a comfortable temperature. Plants, decorative trees, framed art and posters, perhaps even flowers soften, personalize, and enliven the space. Sunlight floods through the windows. The place is humming. One can hear it, see it, and feel it. The library staff will leave tired tonight (exhausted, really) knowing they have worked hard. But they will leave happy, too, knowing that they have done a great job and that hundreds of people are better off today in countless ways, some of which may last a lifetime, because of their efforts. (Fade out to the sound of harps . . . .)

THE HEAVENLY LIBRARIAN, OR, WHAT'S A LIBRARIAN TO DO?

I wish my library could be more like library heaven all the time, for all the students, teachers, staff, and other customers. How can it be made to happen more often, for more people? First, note that library heaven cannot be described without simultaneously describing the librarian and other staff that work there. The library cannot be divorced from the librarian. In the foregoing conceit and in the descriptions from library research that follow, the people who work in libraries and the services they provide go hand in hand. The most perfect facility without the right people doing the right things at the right time for the right customers will not be library heaven.

If you can posit such a thing as library heaven, then imagine what a heavenly librarian must be like. (Library angel?—let's not go there.) Chelton provides a definition of the customer service part of the librarian's job when she writes,

> The theory of practice . . . is idealized as a personal intermediary service available to everyone equally in which librarians/information services staff offer assistance to users in interacting with resources, help provide a link between users and resources, and provide access for users to information, services, and materials (page 7).

What a wonderfully succinct description of the librarian and support staff's job! In library heaven our job is to provide a personal, intermediary service equally to all our customers as they interact with resources. It sounds so simple.

In addition to teaching, library media specialists administer the library media center. That is, we do the parts of the job that, when they are done well, no one notices. Our job is to enable and empower the support staff to make the routine processes of the library run so seamlessly that we are free to attend to professional and administrative tasks, including collaborating with other professionals on specific lessons and consulting with them more broadly as part of curriculum review. With the greater amount of technology and automation in place in today's media centers, school librarians increasingly spend more time and energy working to maintain and support those systems, often not only in the library but throughout the school.

Action Plan #1: Job Description/Job Practice

Find and reread the job description under which you were hired. In one column, jot down the most significant words and phrases in it that relate to customer service. Are there a lot, or relatively few? In another column, note which of these words and phrases specifically target teachers, faculty and/or staff as intended recipients of the library media specialist's services and which ones are aimed more at students. Are you surprised? My own job description mentions service to staff at least a dozen times, about three times as often as direct service to students! Consider the degree to which the services you provide align with the terms of the job description. Does your examination of these points suggest that anything ought to be changed? If so, which should be changed, the job description, the way you are spending your time, or both?

There are times, then, when one begins to feel like the little Dutch boy sticking his fingers in the holes of a leaking dike. There are days when the busy librarian must wonder whether a zenith has been reached in the amount of time and energy he/she is able to devote to the job. That is, has a point of diminishing returns been reached where attempts to do it all are causing some parts of the job to suffer? At times like this it is helpful to get back to basics and remember our professional mission and goals. The "bible" of school library media specialists, *Information Power: Building Partnerships for Learning* (American Association of School Librarians and Association for Educational Communications and Technology, 1998: 100), lists ten principles of school library program administration. These principles clearly delineate many of the major issues that must be addressed to provide customers with excellent library service. Some point the way to improve services already being provided. Some point instead toward pitfalls to be avoided. Consider how each of the following principles reflect customer service issues that must be resolved for library heaven to occur:

Principle 1: The library media program supports the mission, goals, objectives, and continuous improvement of the school.

Principle 2: In every school, a minimum of one full-time, certified/licensed library media specialist supported by qualified staff is fundamental to the implementation of an effective library media program at the building level.

Principle 3: An effective library media program requires a level of professional and support staffing that is based upon a school's instructional programs, services, facilities, size, and numbers of students and teachers.

Principle 4: An effective library media program requires ongoing administrative support.

Principle 5: Comprehensive and collaborative long-range strategic planning is essential to the effectiveness of the library media program.

Principle 6: Ongoing assessment for improvement is essential to the vitality of an effective library media program.

Principle 7: Sufficient funding is fundamental to the success of the library media program.

Principle 8: Ongoing staff development—both to maintain professional knowledge and skills and to provide instruction in information literacy for teachers, administrators, and other members of the learning community—is an essential component of the library media program.

Principle 9: Clear communication of the mission, goals, functions and impact of the library media program is necessary to the effectiveness of the program.

Principle 10: Effective management of human, financial, and physical resources undergirds a strong library media program.

This list of principles paints another vision of library heaven. One might wish to ask a number of questions about each principle concerning implementation strategies. And one might wish to focus efforts for improvement on one principle or another to achieve particular short-term goals. But taken all together, these ten principles effectively define the broad issues that most school library media centers need to resolve in order to deliver quality library service to their customers. They provide an overview of the job library media specialists are asked to perform. How does this translate into day-to-day activity in the library?

Because librarians are teachers, a primary goal is to help customers to learn to do those things that they can for themselves. Of course the library media specialist will assist them as they work to acquire the facts, information, or material they came to get, but equal emphasis is also put on their acquisition of improved skills and knowledge so that they will be able to work more independently the next time they use the library. They should be able to apply their skills in a variety of new situations whether in their classroom, the computer lab, at home, or a public library. Traditionally librarians have not spent a great deal of time and energy in testing student learning, but have provided time for practice and to obtain additional support as needed. This assessment piece of the educational process is going to become more important in the coming years, as various constituencies can be expected to demand greater accountability and the measurement of specific learning outcomes. Benchmarks, rubrics, and standards will become ever more important tools in the assessment of student achievement and the evaluation of library media programs.

CUSTOMER SERVICE IN SCHOOLS: SHORT AND SHORTER

Chelton's study indicates that work with young adults in libraries tends to be characterized by many short interactions with lots of different people about lots of things, few of which might traditionally be called "information services" according to the published standards of library theory.

> Over half (54.9%) of all the librarian encounters are 20 seconds or less, and over four-fifths (82.4%) are under a minute in length (page 129).

Yes, many library contacts with students are short. When in the stacks to do readers' advisory work with students, extended conversations with them about books they might enjoy can (and do) take place. Over time, relationships develop with the students who are seen most frequently. Especially when pleased with the results of earlier encounters, students tend to come in and request help again and again from the same adult, whether that person is the library media specialist or a member of the support staff. Success builds trust and breeds additional requests.

No matter how you look at it, library heaven cannot happen without sufficient staff that is talented, trained, and dedicated. (See Chapter 3 for further discussion of support staff and Figures 2-1 and 2-2 for sample job descriptions.) The fact is that, to the extent that it is possible, each member of the media staff is trained to step in and do whatever job needs to be accomplished. As members of an instructional team working in close proximity under what are sometimes quite stressful circumstances, it becomes clear that every individual must help out on occasion to make things work. The goal is to allow the library to function with a barely diminished degree of service even when one or another member of the team may be absent. This should be possible even if there may be no substitute, even if some crazy emergency then pops up such as the network going down or extra opportunities for service occur such as a class unexpectedly coming in to work in the library. An excellent support staff enables the librarian, then, to focus time and energy on other areas of customer service such as:

- Teaching: sometimes in the classroom, sometimes in the library media center. Providing intellectual access to the library's materials is a prime concern that must be continuously addressed.

- Collaboration: mostly with teachers, mostly about how to deliver the content they want and need in such a way so that information literacy skills can be integrated into the instructional plan. Those skills that students need first are incorporated early in the year, then reinforced throughout the year via resource-based units of study carried out in the library.
- Readers' Advisory: a traditional, assumed, and vital part of the librarian's job that is a pleasure, but that challenges one to keep reading enough, to stay current enough, and to stay enough in touch with the customer's needs.
- Booktalking: and other reading promotion activities in the school and the greater community, including, for example, coordinating author visits and programs with other youth serving agencies
- Technology Support: the librarian is an instructional leader for the faculty and staff in the use and application of instructional technologies. As the "Alpha-Tech-Person" on staff, the librarian may be responsible for planning, implementing, maintaining, and evaluating the use of these technologies.
- Vision: there has to be a plan for the future; maintaining the status quo is not good enough. Needs must be anticipated and planned for before most of the school staff becomes aware that the needs exist. Collaboration with the administration and key players among the school staff makes success in this area possible.
- Problem Solving and Decision Making: when the situation is unique, the librarian gets to make the call.
- Selection and Weeding: the librarian is charged with developing and maintaining a great collection that meets the needs of all the customers.
- Maintaining the Catalog: both physical and intellectual access to the collection via a catalog that is tailored to meet the needs of the young adult customer are essential components of quality service.
- Administration of the Library Media Center and Supervision of Support Staff: ongoing, dynamic, flexible customer-service oriented processes that make or break the library in terms of customer service.

No matter how you say it, library heaven is a place that students, teachers, support staff, administrators, parents, community members—all the customers and potential customers of the school library media center— would be happy and welcome to use. Excellent instruction about how to use the facility and its collections is a given; the collection is rich and

Figure 2–1: Job Description:
South East *Library Media Secretary*

General Description. The library media secretary assists the library media specialist to ensure the smooth and efficient operation of the library media center in providing access to the facility and collections. The secretary works under the direction of the library media specialist, but the formal evaluation is the responsibility of the principal.

Qualifications:
General knowledge of and experience using computers, including word processing ability
Secretarial, clerical, computer or library experience preferred
Appreciation of adolescents and their diverse needs
Ability to relate to and work with diverse population of students and adults
Energy and flexibility; ability to prioritize tasks and complete them expeditiously and accurately
Evidence of good organizational skills
Eager to provide excellent customer service in a helpful, friendly manner

Specific Responsibilities:

I. Library Media Center Maintenance and Operations
   1. Manage circulation functions (sorting and printing lists, notices for overdues and materials)
   2. Assist in keeping the library media center orderly and accessible, including shelving and shelf-reading
   3. Assist students and teachers at circulation desk
   4. Assist in preparation of displays
   5. Maintain library supplies
   6. Prepare materials for bindery

II. Clerical Service
   1. Prepare requisitions for orders, complete processing and accessioning of all new acquisitions (supplies, equipment, and materials) and maintain accurate records, reconciling LMC budget with district statements
   2. Assist with mail/correspondence
   3. Answer telephone, and use fax machine
   4. Handle collection and accounting of fine/lost materials money
   5. Enter data as needed to update and maintain various databases, including circulation/catalog system, consideration file, AUP, bibliographies, etc.
   6. Schedule, distribute, and return resources sent from or borrowed from Grant Wood AEA, District Media, and other agencies; maintain appropriate records as needed
   7. Maintains files of catalogs for print and non-print materials

III. Customer Service
   1. Assist students and teachers in locating materials
   2. Provide basic reference service, when possible, in absence of librarian

3. Assist users with computers, copy machine, and audio-visual equipment
4. Fill reserve and interlibrary loan requests, maintaining necessary records

IV. Audiovisual and Production Services
1. Maintain schedule for reservation of A-V equipment; circulate, and maintain that equipment
2. Provide prompt troubleshooting and repair (or substitution) of A-V equipment that malfunctions, sending it to the district technician for further diagnosis and repair when necessary
3. Assist students and teachers by setting up and demonstrating the use of A-V equipment as needed
4. Record and duplicate video programs as requested within copyright guidelines
5. Operate "Channel One"
6. Maintain A-V supplies/inventory
7. Assist students and staff in laminating and other production tasks using available tools and resources

V. Supervision
1. Remind students of appropriate behavior in library media center, referring problems to the library media specialist or other teachers/staff as appropriate
2. Assist with the training and supervision of student assistants when/if they are recruited
3. Assist the library media specialist and/or teachers providing instruction to students

VI. Other tasks as assigned by library media specialist

Figure 2–2: Job Description:
South East *Library Media Associate*

General Description. The library media associate assists the library media specialist to ensure the smooth and efficient operation of the library media center in providing access to the facility and collections. The associate works under the direction of the library media specialist, but the formal evaluation is the responsibility of the principal.

Qualifications:
General knowledge of and experience using computers, including word processing ability
Secretarial, clerical, computer or library experience preferred
Appreciation of adolescents and their diverse needs
Ability to relate to and work with diverse population of students and adults
Energy and flexibility; ability to prioritize tasks and complete them expeditiously and accurately
Evidence of good organizational skills
Eager to provide excellent customer service in a helpful, friendly manner

Specific Responsibilities:

I. Library Media Center Services
    1. Operate the circulation computer, assisting customers as needed
    2. Assist customers with the library catalog and other computer-based programs
    3. Assist in keeping the library media center orderly and accessible, including shelving and shelf-reading
    4. Assist in preparation of displays
    5. Report needed library supplies to media secretary in sufficient time to allow uninterrupted use
    6. Examine materials for damage and repairs when possible; report replacement needs to library media specialist
    7. Assist in preparing new materials for circulation

II. Clerical Service
    1. Answer telephone
    2. Handle collection and accounting of fine/lost materials money
    3. Assist and/or substitute for media secretary as needed
    4. Accession incoming periodicals and maintain the back issues collection
    5. Maintain the pamphlet file
    6. Perform materials inventory annually as directed by library media specialist

III. Customer Service
    1. Assist students and teachers in locating materials
    2. Provide basic reference service, when possible, in absence of librarian
    3. Assist users with computers, copy machine, and audio-visual equipment
    4. Fill reserve and interlibrary loan requests, maintaining necessary records
    5. Assist students and staff in laminating and using other available production materials

V. Supervision
    1. Collect passes of students coming to the LMC from study hall or classes; maintain an awareness of what students are using the facility and for what purpose; sign passes for students leaving the LMC
    2. Remind students of appropriate behavior in library media center, referring problems to the library media specialist or other teachers/staff as appropriate
    3. Assist with the training and supervision of student assistants when/if they are recruited
    4. Assist the library media specialist and/or teachers providing instruction using computers and software
    5. Assist in the supervision of volunteers

VI. Other tasks as assigned by library media specialist

varied, provides information via many different kinds of media, and meets the needs of the curriculum as well as the customers' leisure reading needs; the facility is flexible enough to meet a wide variety of instructional needs; and the learning that takes place there pays off in increased knowledge and improved performance. Library heaven is hovering there, shimmering just over the horizon. How do we get there? Remember . . .

LIBRARIANS SERVE CUSTOMERS

The library media specialist's main job is to provide services to the customers who come in the door. For students, teachers, support staff, and others, the librarian is a problem solver and doer of good deeds. Our services are wide ranging, and vary significantly from one school library media center to the next, from one region or state to another, and from the younger end of the young adult age range served in seventh and eighth grade libraries to the older end served in high school libraries.

Circulation, however, is a service that is probably much the same from one place to the next. It may be the library's most visible service, and is likely the one thing that most people think about when libraries or librarians come to mind. With a student population of around 800, the South East Junior High library circulates an average of just under 20,000 items per school year. Materials circulate to students, primarily, but also to teachers, administrators, parents, and sometimes to the general public. No fines are charged for overdues, as this would seem to consume more staff time and energy than it would be worth. Fines are assessed for damage to materials that is judged to have been deliberate or as a result of carelessness, and for lost materials.

Ironically, while the stereotype that most people carry around in their heads is that of a librarian as someone who sits at the counter checking out books, this is a function that the school library media specialist with at least some support staff seldom has the opportunity to enjoy. And because it is primarily at the circulation desk that one might naturally learn customers' names, it can be difficult for the librarian to establish close, personal, "first-name" ties with very many students. Thus one must be fairly assertive in asking for the customers' names in other situations to build that degree of familiarity and friendliness that can contribute so positively to reader's advisory and other library customer service interactions.

Some other services provided in a school library media center, such as reference service, are roughly analogous to that provided in a public library. At the South East Junior High library, at least, and in school library media centers generally, I believe, reference service is less frequent and less formal than the reference service typically provided at the public library. Why?

REFERENCE SERVICE IN THE SCHOOL LIBRARY MEDIA CENTER

There are relatively few times that a customer walks into the school library media center with a specific reference question that can be answered by a relatively simple search in a standard reference source. It simply doesn't happen every day. And there is certainly no time that the librarian, as the information professional in the library, is sitting at a desk for the exclusive purpose of answering such questions.

Some interesting reference questions come through the door, of course, like the student who wanted to know how many square inches of Disneyland there are. It was simple enough once we found a source that told us its size in some measurement of area, to find the necessary conversion formula, and to convert the answer to square inches. There are also assignment specific reference questions that one finds repeated from one year to the next. For example, a social studies teacher has a packet in which one member of each group is assigned to find the price of flax in Virginia in the early eighteenth century. There is one print source of this information in my library that I am aware of, a document from the Census Bureau published as part of the U.S. bicentennial celebration of 1976 (and I have recently seen similar information on the Internet). Another example is the PE teachers who give extra credit assignments such as the one asking students to report on the differences between the swimming events at the NCAA championships and at the Olympic competitions, including the current record times for each. It always takes a few minutes to recall that, although part of the answer can be found in the *World Almanac*, the rest must be found in a couple of other sports books in the general collection.

Molly R. Pederson's article "Sermon from the Stacks" encapsulates beautifully a concept that is critical to providing good reference service to young adults in any library: that "Even if you cannot take a reference question seriously, you must always take the patron asking it seriously" (1999: 56-57). That is, respect the customer.

But it seems possible that there are some days when no single reference question happens to walk in the door. These days may be the equivalent of public librarians who scream that they are *so* sick and tired of telling people where the bathroom is. Depending on what students happen to be doing in their classrooms on a given day, depending on what assignments have been given and when they are due, there are some days of relative quiet when students' reference questions are very few and far between. Students will ask who wrote a particular book, or ask what was the title of book that was mentioned in a previous booktalk in so-and-so's class six days (or weeks) before. They will ask where such and such is located, or ask for permission or access to one thing or another. They have problems with the computers and questions about printing and photocopying. There are equipment problems in the production room and lots of things going on to keep the entire library staff busy. But traditional reference work of the type taught in reference classes in schools of library and information science may be a relatively infrequent occurrence unless classes are present doing research.

Students and other school personnel ask for all these other kinds of service because they perceive that the librarian and the library support staff is available, knowledgeable, and exists primarily to serve them. It is easier for the customer to ask for help than it is to look up the information in the computer catalog. Or perhaps they've lost the bibliography they were given in class. This type of service shades more into readers' advisory work than reference, and forces one to consider how much more teaching one should do to the customers about how to do their own work rather than merely serving as a reference librarian who quickly and easily answers the presenting problem. And since readers' advisory in all its permutations is the bedrock reason many librarians decided to get into the library profession, one must try never to mind being "interrupted" to answer these kinds of questions. Providing the right book to the right reader at the right time remains one of the school library media specialist's favorite challenges.

Teachers, by the way, also rarely ask standard reference questions. There might be one or two per week on average from a staff of 40+ full-time teachers. Instead, most need general help finding what's available on a curricular topic or perhaps locating a video that will work with a particular unit. Again, these are not, strictly speaking, reference questions. Instead, they represent another kind of access that as school library media specialist one needs to provide.

Formal, grown-up, big-time worries like money and health and life-and-death subjects are seldom the subjects of reference questions in the school library media center. There are exceptions, such as the student who said that his dad had just been diagnosed with cancer and wanted more information on the disease; there was a girl who said she was trying to decide which of her two step-families to live with and wondered if there was statistical information about blended families that might help her make up her mind. But most questions, instead, are to provide depth, interest, or verisimilitude to the writing or research being performed by students. These questions come completely out of left field. Students enjoy testing the collection and the librarian's knowledge of it. Assiduous writer/scholars can regularly surprise, delight, and occasionally stump the unwary librarian. But in any case, the task of the library media specialist is, again, to find the best balance between providing the right answers for the student and teaching them how to find the answers for themselves. It is exactly the same question one faces when providing reference assistance to members of the faculty and staff. Again, the questions to be instantly assessed have to do with the amount of time both the customer and the media specialist have, what skills or knowledge must come into play, and the extent to which the best service can be provided by simply providing the answer versus teaching the customer how to do it. Using the computer, for example, makes one consider under what circumstances the librarian should put hands on the mouse or keyboard and when the customer should take or retain control. Some practitioners would say to always let the customer be in control. In practice there are some times when in the short term it is better to get the job done as quickly as possible so that the customer can get about the business of using the information instead of spending all the available time simply trying to find it. It really is a small but somewhat delicate matter about which each librarian must make a judgment call each time the opportunity for such service presents itself. In general, if one must err, let it be on the side of leaving the control in the hands of the customer. Teach them to fish for themselves whenever possible.

ADDITIONAL/TRADITIONAL SERVICES

Students, teachers, and other staff customers need support in the production of materials for instruction. Supplies of traditional "paper and pencil" sorts of materials such as poster board, drawing, construction and bulletin board paper, glue and glue sticks, markers, rulers, scissors, etc., are routinely provided. Paper cutters, a laminating machine, counter space, and tables provide workspace so that students and staff can create what is needed. A punch binder for making plastic spiral bound books may still be in use, but so may be audio and/or video production materials such as a supply of tapes, equipment including analog and digital recorder/players, cameras, editing equipment, and attendant microphones, production facilities, etc. In the last decade, increased access to computers and printers (ink jet, laser, and now color laser) make the production of increasingly sophisticated paper stuff possible. And read/write CD-ROMs are now economical and reliable enough to make "burning" the customer's data practical.

Of course production in the school library media center now may also include nonprint products such as computer presentations in PowerPoint©, Hyperstudio©, databases and spreadsheets. It can also mean audio and/or videotapes. In the latter case, editing, special effects, and character generation using analog and/or digital editing equipment is possible.

Service includes helping students and teachers with interlibrary loan requests. Whether the request is from a student, teacher, or other staff member for personal reading or for a curricular need, borrowing the requested item from another collection is a small but important way to show respect for the customer. If the customer has easy access to the local public library, it may be possible to go online to check their catalog for copy availability. In some locales, the customer may be able to place these items on hold via the online system, and may be checked out for delivery to the school. That's customer service!

LIBRARIANS CREATE AND MANAGE THE ENVIRONMENT FOR CUSTOMER SERVICE

In a recent *Booklist* column, Michael Cart reminisced about libraries he has known and loved. He described the feelings invoked by a favorite spot in a favorite library, recalling it as being, " . . . a place that banishes darkness and its demons, a place that is unfailingly snug and secure, a place that is . . . well, sanctuary" (2000: 1,538). Is it too much to ask that the school library media center be configured so that it can provide customers with a feeling of sanctuary? No, this aspiration is not beyond reach. While the ideal library media center will be active, a bustling place of learning, for at least some customers it can also be a place of refuge.

For most students most of the time school is really a pretty OK place. They get along with others, learn more or less what they should learn, and find ways to get through their days with a minimum of fuss or trouble. For some students, school is actually fabulous—not that they'd like to admit it. It is challenging, exciting, they get to spend a fair amount of their time with their friends, and they find plenty of things to engage their interest.

But put yourself in the shoes of a student who may not be terribly successful in the classroom. It's easy to imagine that he (for the sake of example) dreads coming to school in general. He plots out his day in terms of which classes he expects to be intolerable and those few that he hopes may merely make him uncomfortable. Imagine that on most days he can finagle a way to go to the library for at least a few minutes. Imagine that when he gets there he is greeted in a friendly way. Nobody asks him to answer any embarrassing questions in front of his classmates. There is no homework to turn in and none will be assigned. There are no tests to take. Instead, he is the one who gets to ask the questions. The adults on duty answer his questions personally, taking the time to tell him and often to show him how to do or get or find what he wants. There are comfortable chairs to sit in instead of desks in rows as are in most classrooms. There is carpeting on the floor instead of tile. Bright windows flood the plants with light and the walls are decorated with posters and art. The room is fairly large, big enough so that when he wants to he can walk around and stretch a bit. Sure, the place is full of books and these may not be his thing. But there may be a person who works in the library who, over time, he begins to enjoy talking with—maybe about books, but more likely, in his case, about some other interest area like computer games, some magazine he likes to read, the weather, his weekend, sports—almost anything. Wouldn't that begin to feel a little like a haven? Wouldn't it provide a kind of sanctuary? Couldn't it be another slice of library heaven?

People, policies, and procedures each play their part in creating this kind of warm and supportive environment. But it is also important to consider the role of the physical space the library inhabits. The layout of the school library media center can assist the staff in providing equitable, high-quality library service, or it can create barriers. Creating and managing the interior space that makes up one's library media center is probably more often the result of luck (good or bad) than anything else. But it is important because customers, such as the above-mentioned Mr. Cart, may carry an impression of the look and feel of a place long after memories of actual library service or those who provided them have faded. And yes, there could be a future *Booklist* columnist using your library today. Even more likely, there may be a future city council member, principal, mayor, school board member, state or federal legislator, or library board member—and surely several hundreds or thousands of individual voters—whose decisions may someday influence the quality, not to say the very existence, of the library you hold so dear. The feelings they have about the services you provide may be the most important thing you leave with them.

Ask yourself: Does the physical layout help the library media center achieve its mission? Are the colors, graphics, and decorative items (art) conducive to study, reflection, learning, fun, and exploration? Are materials arranged for easy physical access as well as adequate control? One way to find out is to assume the role of your customers and see how things work.

Considering the entire scheme of how the media center is arranged and the range of services it provides, how can both the literal and figurative paths the student must follow be made as direct and painless as possible? Efficiency is the goal. Does the student need to have a pass signed upon arriving in the library or only when leaving? Who will do this? Is this person likely to be found along the path the student will follow or will this simple and oft-repeated task require that they take a detour?

Action Plan #2: Role Playing

How do customers move around in your library? The flow of traffic should be examined from a number of different perspectives—literally. Role-playing can be a useful tool to examine aspects of your library's physical environment. Imagine, for example, that you are a student coming to the library for . . . what? Begin by making a list of as many different things as you can think of that students might want to do when they come to your library media center. Just as a starting point, they might want to:

- Return a book
- Use the catalog
- Check out a book
- Read a magazine
- Use the Internet
- Do some word processing
- Use the copy machine
- Print something from a floppy disk
- Research using an encyclopedia or other reference materials
- Work on a small group project
- Return or pick up a piece of AV equipment for a teacher

Use this task list to look for efficient use of time and space. Make a similar task list for other library customers, such as teachers, associates, and other support personnel. At what points do these various customers' needs conflict? Can the physical environment be managed to provide better service by reducing such conflicts?

If the student is unable to accomplish the task at hand independently, from whom might they get help? Is this person nearby or at least in sight? If a staff member is temporarily out of his/her normal position, who covers for them in the meantime?

To what extent can the student accomplish their task without interfering with other ongoing activities in the facility? Are particular areas of the room intended for particular kinds of uses and are these areas discernable? If/when students or other customers are acting inappropriately in one of these areas, who is in the best position to deal with them in a positive, proactive, fair, and courteous way?

Answering questions such as these may help you find ways to improve customer service without adding any additional staff, with minimal additional training, and at low cost. But before you make a big change you might also want to consider doing some . . .

Observation

Without being too obvious about it, observe a student as they go about their tasks to see how things actually work. Examine the differences between what you expected and what you actually saw happen and think about the causes and effects of those differences. Are there things you can change to make things work better, more easily, or efficiently?

Similarly, generate a list of tasks that teachers, associates, and other frequent customers of your library media center come to accomplish. Take a few minutes to pretend that you are that teacher coming in to the library to check out a camcorder or to use the phone. Or imagine that you are an associate coming to laminate materials in the back room while supervising a special education student or two and try to walk around in that associate's shoes. Which library staff members do they need to talk with? Where are the supplies they need to use? What kinds of problems do they encounter that could be improved by better signage, by relocating materials to a different location, or by other manipulations of the physical space that is available? Who should they see if they have problems? Is that person located so as to be able to provide the desired service as easily as possible, without undo "collisions" with other staff or customers who might be doing other things?

In designing a new building, architects go through a schematic design phase in which they examine the kinds of tasks being done, how they relate to each other, and consider the size of the room in relation to factors such as sound, lighting, heating, and air conditioning. They go on to consider how this space will relate to adjacent spaces. Even in retrospect—that is, looking at a building or library space that is already in place—this sort of schematic design analysis can be useful to ensure that, to as great an extent as possible, the physical environment is not working at cross-purposes with the tasks the staff, students, and library staff are trying to accomplish. Rather than creating conflict where people are bumping into each other trying to get things done, one hopes that the physical facility will develop a kind of synergy, a melding of people and tasks that contributes to the accomplishment of individual goals that is greater than the sum of its parts.

OTHER CONSIDERATIONS

Appearance

Look at the physical layout of the media center to see if it welcomes customers. Consider ways in which the layout can help make the customer feel comfortable, capable, and secure. For example, does the entry area somehow say "library" so that the first-time user knows he/she is in the right place? This can also benefit the repeat customer, who is reminded upon each visit that he/she is leaving one place (whether that is the hall, the street, or a classroom, etc.) and entering another place, the library. Use of color, arrangement of furniture, and other fixtures can contribute to a feeling of comfort or ease. Signage that is clear, easy to read, and helpful can make the customer more independent and contribute to his/her feeling of competence. Placement of staff desks so that the staff remains visible and accessible to the customer while working can help make the customer secure in the knowledge that assistance, should they need it, is available nearby. The use of staff name tags makes them more easily recognizable as library employees and can allow the customer to more easily call them by name, personalizing interactions and building fleeting, but potentially important relationships. And as mentioned elsewhere, staff training in policies and procedures that enhance positive customer relations complete the picture of a library that is positive and serious about providing the best possible customer service.

In a school library media center, having open "line-of-sight" control of as much of the area as possible is especially important. Although there are times that special circumstances make it difficult, the library is always staffed by at least one adult. Whenever possible, that adult supervisor is in the front/main room, visible to anyone who is in the library or who may enter the library. Convex "security mirrors" can be placed to permit staff to see areas of the room that would otherwise be blocked from view. Customers seem to be of two minds about the mirrors: Some

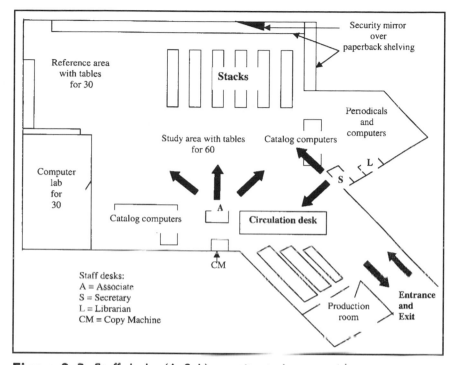

Figure 2–3: Staff desks (A, S, L) are situated to provide easy access to staff members by the customer. Line-of-sight control of the facility from the desks of library staff members contributes greatly to effective customer service in the school library (arrows). Security mirror at far wall above paperback shelving provides a view of "blind spots" in back of the stacks. Windows (not shown) provide a view into the computer lab, which is supervised by the teacher using it.

forget that the mirrors are there, perhaps due to their ubiquity in the retail environment, and are amazed when the mirrors allow the staff to see things that they thought were being done in private. Other customers are aware of the presence of the mirror and consciously modify their behavior because they assume we can see them at all times. Either way, the library benefits. A third, less desirable effect, may be that the mirror implies a lack of trust and communicates the idea that we are trying to "catch" our customers doing something wrong. When this issue is raised (usually by a staff member, not a student) mention is made of the fact that the library is liable for the safety of all its customers and that the mirrors make it possible for the staff to maintain better supervision than would otherwise be possible.

Traffic Patterns

Although the shortest distance between two points is a straight line, a curving or circular traffic pattern may be desirable in the library. The majority of people are right-handed. Vehicles, including the bikes many of our young YA customers ride, are driven in the right-hand lane. So a traffic pattern that brings customers into the facility on the right side and moves them through the facility in a counterclockwise circular flow so that they exit along the right-hand side proves comfortable and convenient for most customers. Notice how this pattern does nothing to impede other customers who might be coming into the library.

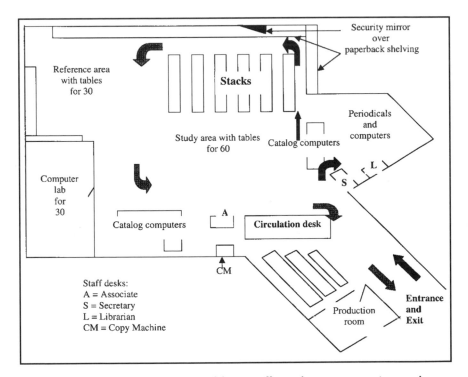

Figure 2–4: A circular pattern of foot traffic reduces congestion and conflict. Most "drop-in" students (as opposed to those who are with a class) move from the catalog computers to the stacks, especially to the paperbacks, before circling back to the circulation desk to check out. Others turn right to the current periodicals and computers. Classes most often use the reference area and the computer lab. The copy machine is near the associate's desk to provide better customer assistance.

Siting Collections

Given a particular physical environment, consider how collections may best be sited for maximum use. The most popular materials, such as paperbacks or magazines, might be placed for easiest access. Another library might find it best to place these same materials to take advantage of their visual impact. Another institution might prefer to use them to attract the customers to a particular part of the facility that otherwise is underutilized. Similarly, reference materials might best be used in the quietest, low traffic area. But that doesn't mean that another library might prefer to have them close to the circulation desk to facilitate the work of the staff in assisting users with these materials. Experiment to determine how various areas of the facility might best be used to meet the needs of individual, small group, whole-class, and/or larger group instruction. Can teaching tools such as a black or white board, an overhead, computer with network connections and a digital projector, etc., be used as needed with each of these audiences?

Most librarians will prefer to locate the most commonly used tools and materials where they will be quickly and easily available, both in terms of their actual distance and their perceived distance or line-of-sight from the entrance. At South East Junior High these "close-in" features would include the circulation desk, computer catalog workstations, fiction, new-book displays, and paperbacks. There is also an "off-ramp" to the right for current issues of magazines, some consumables, "drop-in" computers for word processing, and comfortable chairs. Customers whose needs are met in these parts of the library can be in and out and on their way in a very short period of time and with minimal disturbance to others who are in the library for different tasks. The librarian's desk and computer and those of the library secretary are also in this area. This increases the likelihood that at least one of them will be present in this high traffic area most of the time. The highly transient and independent nature of the tasks performed in this area also make it a worthwhile area for direct supervision.

Customers need to go a bit deeper to get to the nonfiction shelving, computers with the full complement of electronic databases, reference, story collections, and biographies. The attempt is to match the placement of the material in a way that it is related to how the customer is most like to use it. So, for example, the hustle and bustle and talking that must go on around the circulation desk is near the entrance. As far away from that as possible is the reference area, where customers might be expected to work over an extended period of time in relative quiet. This is also the place where whole-class instruction most often takes place.

Another aspect of the physical environment is a consideration of the location of the people (student assistants, secretary, and librarian) in the facility. Are they located so that they are accessible to the customers who need their services? Are sight lines such that needy customers can see the person who can help them, recognize which individual they need, and approach them without undue difficulty? An office, a place to pile and file the mountains of paperwork that still pour into the library every day is still necessary. But having the librarian's desk, complete with networked computer and phone, out on the floor of the library makes it possible to do quite a bit of desk work—albeit in fits and starts— while maintaining a great sense of accessibility to the customers. If these kinds of work were done out of sight, back in an enclosed office, it might be possible to get more work done, but it would be invisible and the librarian would be invisible. The librarian's computer also can be made available as an additional workstation on those occasions when every other computer in the room is in use by students.

FURNITURE

Yes, furniture has an impact on customer service. Functionality is of primary importance. But also consider that furniture such as tables and chairs should be comfortable and that it should match the rest of the library in color, style, and material so that it contributes to a harmonious overall appearance. A balance must be achieved between the need that furniture be sturdy enough to withstand frequent and almost continuous hard use while at the same time being comfortable enough to welcome customers and make their stay at least bearable, if not downright pleasant.

As public libraries sometimes provide "remote" drop-off boxes at grocery stores or other locations apart from the main library, school libraries sometimes find it worthwhile to provide a drop box in locations away from the library that are more convenient for the students. This might be near the main office, entry lobby, or school lunchroom, for example. The added convenience this service might provide to the customer must be weighed against the additional labor of regularly servicing these drop-off points. In addition, one might find an increase in sturm and drang when customers allege that they returned the book to the remote drop box and somebody must have stolen it.

SIGNAGE

Signs can be designed to reflect a customer service attitude. For example consider the difference between a sign that says, "**STOP!** No Students beyond this point!!!" versus a kinder, gentler one that says, "**Staff work area:** Please ask staff before using this area." Which sign, placed on a computer, would a teen feel best reading: "Not for student use!" or "Not for student use without staff permission"? The former seems abrupt, harsh, and arbitrary. The latter leaves room for talking or negotiation and shows greater respect for the customer.

BULLETIN BOARDS AND OTHER DISPLAYS

Can bulletin boards or displays be designed to reflect a positive customer service attitude? Other means of promoting the library such as electronic signs, in-house or cable TV productions, or even Web pages could be scrutinized to ensure that the message being delivered to the customer is a positive and welcoming one.

Color can effectively enhance the mood of the library. Unfortunately, you probably won't be given much, if any, choice in the selection of the color of important features like the paint on the walls or the carpet or other floor covering. Others will probably make these decisions and they may or may not solicit or accept your input. Don't sweat the small stuff, even if it is not really small stuff. Do the things you can and let the rest go. Share some catalogs of promotional materials such as ALA Graphic's "READ" posters with your teen customers and let them choose some items for purchase and display.

In an editorial entitled "Soothing Words Often Begin with 'L'" Leonard Kniffel contemplated the mental or intellectual mood that a library can engender. He wrote, "A good library represents an island of tranquility, balance, sanity, and reason in a tumultuous world, whether that world is a business, a school, a community, or a home. But a library is not merely an escape from chaos or isolation; it is the entrance to other worlds, thoughts, times, and minds, and it's a place where you are likely to find others who yearn for the fresh air of intellectual engagement" (1999: 34).

That the library can be a kind of community where one might find comfort not only in the collections but also in the like-minded people encountered there is another slice of library heaven. While the setting, design, style, furnishings, materials, and other aspects of the physical space that comprises the library media center and its physical environment are certainly open to infinite interpretations, the functions which are to be accomplished are fairly immutable. The tools change, the goals remain the same. School library media specialists need to find ways to make the physical environment of the facility become a contributing factor to the accomplishment of the educational goals of the library. The

space and the furniture and the traffic patterns and the surface treat-
ments and lights and heating and air conditioning should each work in
favor of the customers and the staff.

LIBRARIANS DEVELOP, MAINTAIN, AND CIRCULATE THE COLLECTION FOR CUSTOMERS

Sometimes students ask me if I've read every book in the library. I always laugh and shake my head no, but allow that I work hard to know
the collection and have read many of the books in it. How much reading does that take? I tell my graduate students in my course "Library
Materials for Young Adults" that if they want to stay current in YA literature they should read a YA book a day. They gasp and I add that if
they can't read three to four YA books per week they are probably in
the wrong business. Those who can, do. Those who can't go into reference (with apologies to Will Manley).

Other students sometimes ask if I know everything. Of course I give
them the standard answer, "No, but I try to know as much as I can about
where to find information about anything." Providing excellent customer
service means that we will do our best. We will give the customer and
his/her request as much time and energy as possible and the customer
will know what has been done to help them and why. Customer service
means seldom having to say you're sorry (with apologies to *Love Story*.)

Charles Curran and Dennis Adams wrote in "Galloping New Ignorance, Watchdogs, and the Enlightenment Syndrome" that librarians
" . . . select, purchase, classify, organize, store, retrieve, interpret, and
teach the use of print, micro, and electronic information . . ." (1999: 46-
49). That's a good start, but it only begins to describe one aspect of the
library media specialist's job: that having to do with collection management.

Take that first item, "select" as an example and think about how it
impacts customer service. The task is to select and purchase that right
book for the right reader so that it will be available at the right time.
The process begins with the librarian having access to several professional review journals and being familiar enough with them and their
reviewers' styles, preferences, and expertise so that informed purchasing decisions can be made. Reading professional journals is not something that most school librarians can do during the school day, so it is
done at home. Often, especially in the case of expensive multimedia materials or computer software, the librarian needs to work with other members of the school's staff or even a committee to decide whether or not

a particular piece of material will be ordered. Even the best video discs or software materials may languish unused if teachers have not played an active role in their selection. Teachers need to be comfortable with how materials can be used to support their curriculum, and teachers must provide input as to how materials might be used, how many copies should be purchased, and about what format or what delivery method would be best, etc. There may be many decision points and many time-consuming and energy-sapping steps to complete a seemingly simple task like "selecting" an item for the collection.

Purchasing an item for the collection often involves maintaining a consideration list and/or database of materials. In the past this may have consisted of handwritten notecards or other manual means. As microcomputers and database software became readily available, many school librarians shifted their consideration files to this format. Now another shift toward various versions of electronic ordering based on CD-ROM catalogs and online databases seems to be taking hold. Maintaining this consideration database and using it to order the desired materials for the collection is still a time-consuming and exacting task. Depending on one's individual situation, one might need to submit orders to meet particular order dates; orders might need to be formatted in particular ways; orders might be submitted by the central office in a timely and accurate manner; or orders might now be e-mailed or faxed directly and almost instantly to the vendor.

And then budget matters are a concern. Is there enough money in the budget to buy the items one needs? If one buys an encyclopedia, should it be print or electronic? Should books be primarily hardbacks to provide access to the latest and greatest that is only available in that format? Or should one stretch those limited dollars to the max by buying primarily multiple, cheaper copies of paperback books which are so clearly preferred by most young adult readers? Should one order popular periodicals that may find an audience or those most likely to be needed for research? Does purchasing an online periodical database allow you to cancel certain print subscriptions? Should you buy a new computer for the library catalog or three boomboxes, two VCRs, and a digital camera? The questions, decisions, and sticking points can seem endless.

Classification of the collection and organization go hand in hand. While many librarians regard cataloging class as a kind of yardstick of pain by which all other classes may be measured, we nonetheless recognize the critical role of accurate, inspired cataloging in providing access to our collections. Many school librarians now purchase cataloging for most materials, but many, especially in smaller, more rural schools, still create original cataloging for at least some of the items they select. Some school districts employ a district cataloger who does the bulk of the work, but even then individual librarians may find it necessary to tweak certain records to fit their school's particular needs. Creating, maintaining, and teaching the use of one's catalog is critical to the success of the library media center and it is a constant, ongoing task. Errors creep into the system and have to be fixed. Students use the catalog in increasingly sophisticated ways as the year goes on, while new students drop in who know nothing about it and may have to start learning from scratch.

Storing and retrieving items in the collection similarly go hand in hand. Librarians are responsible for storing items in the collection in such a way so that they are secure, accessible, won't be easily or unnecessarily damaged, etc. We store different parts of the collection in different ways so that they will be as secure as possible while also being as accessible as they can be to the intended users. All of this is done so that the customer can find, consider, and choose to retrieve the item when it is needed or wanted.

School library media specialists work with customers to interpret the information that has been found. Does anyone assert that students read better today than they did in the past? It is an increasing challenge for school libraries to provide more materials at lower reading levels. In the junior high, it is now necessary to provide materials, especially books, to meet the curricular content students need but also at reading levels two, four, or six years below their grade level. When these students come to the library to work, especially if they are working on their own, considerable time and effort can be spent assisting them in a tutorial or mentoring mode. At the same time, even the most erudite reader or most able teacher sometimes needs assistance in using resources found in computer databases, on the Web, or in print. Helping meet the needs of the diverse learners is an ongoing challenge.

Similarly, students, teachers, and other customers who use school libraries need to learn how to use the information in the collections whatever the format, whether print, micro, or electronic. Librarians have to know not only how to use these formats, but also how to teach others to use them, and frequently how to troubleshoot, repair, and maintain them. Book repair is still a job that has to be done; it's just that computer and printers and all the rest have been added to the mix.

And these are just the first of those many critical steps in building, maintaining, and using a great school library media center collection. Weeding the collection could merit a book in itself, and inventory is a major job that can consume considerable time and energy. The collection development and maintenance tasks described here are only a small part of the job performed by school library media specialists. These tasks are essential to providing good customer service, and they are mostly out of both sight and mind of the customers. I really think that most customers have no idea how the books get on the shelf, and they don't really care. They just want them to be there when they want them. It's our job to do our best to make that happen as often as possible.

ADMINISTRATIVE SUPPORT

Good customer service in a school library media center requires strong, ongoing support by the building principal.

Information Power lists two principles that are particularly relevant to the role of the building's highest administrator: "Principle 4: An effective library media program requires ongoing administrative support" and "Principle 7: Sufficient funding is fundamental to the success of the library media program" (American Association of School Librarians and Association for Educational Communications and Technology, 1998: 100).

Action Plan #3: Bosses

The library media specialist has several "bosses," people who have some direct say over what can be done and how it may be done. Consider each of these people and the impact they have on the delivery of excellent customer service in the school library media center.

On an ongoing, day-to-day basis, the principal is the boss of all school employees. It is she (or her designee) who determines the budget of the library media center. It is she who formally evaluates the performance of every school employee following the process and using the district-approved evaluation instrument. She approves all purchases and is the end of the chain of command in the building concerning personnel, building policy, building activities, etc. To what extent is she informed about what's going on in the library? Is she supportive and aware of current trends and developments? Make a list of ways in which the librarian can support the principal's efforts to improve the school's performance.

In larger districts, another boss is the district media coordinator. She provides guidance and direction for the district's media program. She administers funds such as capital equipment and federal funds

---

Action Plan #3 (*cont.*)

such as Title VI, determining how these will be allocated to each of the library media centers in the district. She plans, schedules, and conducts districtwide media department meetings. She is part of the district Technology Team that decides how to disburse state and district technology funds. She coordinates ordering, is in charge of district cataloging and the district media collection, and coordinates end of year deadlines for media specialists.

Other bosses include members of the central administrative staff such as directors of instruction and, ultimately, the superintendent of schools. They are involved in implementing policy as set by the school board that often bears directly on the librarian's efforts. What opportunities are there to communicate directly with these bosses about media matters?

It is elected citizens serving on the school board without pay who are legally charged with operating the schools, however. They set policy and evaluate the superintendent. They ensure that the schools comply with all state and federal policies, and are the legal entity that hires and fires all school employees, etc. Are they aware of the mission of the school library and the media program? What can the librarian do to make them feel welcome to visit your facility and learn more about your successes as well as your needs?

Remember then, that there is a kind of chain of command that infuses every act of customer service. When we check out a book for a customer, we are serving that customer, supporting the school's mission, fulfilling the duty of the principal, the directors of instruction, the superintendent, and the school board. Ultimately, our circulation of that book serves the people of our community, state, and nation. Not too big a responsibility, is it?

The building principal determines how the ratio of teachers to students will be allocated, which includes whether or not to hire a library media specialist. Ultimately, these decisions about ratio determine class size. The principal decides which programs are provided with associates and how many hours those associates work. He/she decides how the budget is allocated within the building. He/she has some control over the extent to which site-based decision making, including some budgeting decisions, will be made. He/she makes recommendations about the hiring and firing of all building personnel. He/she manages and administers the school in the same way that the library media specialist manages and administers the library media program. Also like the library media specialist, the principal is charged with specific goals, given resources with which to accomplish those goals, and is evaluated on the basis of his/her performance.

TIME

Because time is short for students who visit the library media center, good customer service minimizes any wait time they have, especially at the circulation desk. Unfortunately, one may find that there are times when the circulation desk, the heart of customer service in the school library media center, is unstaffed. Sometimes a person is absent; more often they may have been called away to the phone, are running an errand elsewhere in the building, are taking a break, shelving books, assisting a customer elsewhere in the library, or are helping with the copy machine, a computer, or printer, etc. Chelton's research suggests that teens feel slighted and quickly get irritable when they feel they are waiting for service. Therefore, she recommends that libraries,

> . . . keep unexplained waiting to an absolute minimum or learn how to 'explain' the wait so that the adolescent user does not feel ignored by the service provider (page 204).

Each person who works at the circulation desk, whether staff or student assistants, needs to be aware of and sensitive to the needs of the customers—not only adolescent users but to all the library media center's customers. Nobody likes to wait, although some highly evolved people are better at it than others. Experience suggests that as long as people have enough time and can see that progress is being made toward getting to the front of the line, they are patient and polite and the usual procedure works. But let someone get a little testy (as happens more frequently on the last day before a vacation break, or the last day of a grading period, for example) and all of a sudden no one is happy. When a large number of customers are waiting in line to check out materials at the circulation desk, relief may be provided by temporarily opening another computer workstation for circulation. Even if it takes a minute to bring that second workstation up, students will appreciate that the library staff has noticed the long line and is working to help them as quickly as possible. Most circulation desk encounters are short, from ten to sixty seconds. While waiting in line, students converse and look at counter displays, select bookmarks, retrieve their passes, and ponder the

"READ" posters hanging behind and over the circulation desk. They generally seem to enjoy the few minutes of "down time" during which they can visit quietly with their friends or with other library staff in the area. On those few occasions when irritation or anxiety is evident, a brief intervention—"I'm sorry you had to wait. Can I sign that pass for you?"—seems to ameliorate most negative feelings. Within a couple of minutes the two stations can handle ten to twenty circulation transactions and everyone is on their way.

When only one person is on duty in the library (such as when other staff is out to teach, supervise a study hall, at lunch, or otherwise called away) problems can develop. There are times when the librarian is hammering away at e-mail and notices that a student is standing nearby or even waiting over at the circulation desk, hoping to be noticed. Some students ask (timidly or otherwise) for help. Others just wait without speaking. Apologizing for not having noticed them earlier and advising them that they need to make more noise next time seems to make them feel better. They usually laugh nervously and nod their heads, but are they really any more likely to do that should the same circumstance arise? It is hard to know. It is fortunate that this really does not happen very often. In most cases, a student assistant or other library staff member is on duty at the circulation desk. And if the student assistant is not present (ill, busy elsewhere in the library, or performing a duty out of the library) the library media center associate or secretary is frequently nearby and available to help.

Good signage could help, though. A small sign at the desk might say, "Please look around the room to see who is available. There IS an adult here who will be happy to help you!" or "Please excuse the wait. We'll help you as soon as we can." The truth is that many students fail to see or read such signs, but it might help in at least some cases. And it seems to me that asking the customer to look around the room and find an adult to help them is better than leaving them completely uninformed.

REFERENCES

American Association of School Librarians and Association for Educational Communications and Technology. 1998. *Information Power: Building Partnerships for Learning.* Chicago: American Library Association and Washington, DC: Association for Educational Communications and Technology.

Cart, Michael. 2000. "A Clean, Well Lighted Sanctuary." *Booklist* (April 15): 1,538.

Chelton, Mary K. 1997. *Adult-Adolescent Service Encounters: The Library Context.* Ph.D. dissertation. New Brunswick, NJ: Rutgers University.

Curran, Charles, and Dennis Adams. 1999. "Galloping New Ignorance, Watchdogs, and the Enlightenment Syndrome." *American Libraries* (November): 46–49.

Kniffel, Leonard. 1999. "Soothing Words Often Begin with 'L' ". *American Libraries* (November): 34.

Pederson, Molly R. 1999. "Sermon from the Stacks." *American Libraries* (October): 56–57.

Chapter 3

Library Support Staff

Joel Shoemaker

Information Power: Building Partnerships for Learning has this to say about library staff in its list of "Principles of Program Administration":

> Principle 2: In every school, a minimum of one full-time, certified/licensed library media specialist supported by qualified staff is fundamental to the implementation of an effective library media program at the building level.

> Principle 3: An effective library media program requires a level of professional and support staffing that is based upon a school's instructional programs, services, facilities, size, and numbers of students and teachers.

> Principle 8: Ongoing staff development—both to maintain professional knowledge and skills and to provide instruction in information literacy for teachers, administrators, and other members of the learning community—is an essential component of the library media program (American Association of School Librarians and Association for Educational Communications and Technology, 1998: 100).

It cannot be said too often: the library staff is the single most critical element in providing excellent customer service in a school library. A similarly strong case is made for the importance of library staff and support staff in *Directions for Library Services to Young Adults*:

Good policies will not result in better service if young adults encounter hostility or distrust in the library. The essential ingredient
is a public service staff with tolerance for youthful exuberance and
for differing lifestyles and clothing styles. Sympathetic and knowledgeable staff, in combination with building, collection, and service design factors, make for a congenial library . . ." (Young Adult Library
Services Association, 1993: 7)

And a congenial library is a good step toward a customer-service oriented library. With good collections, good policies, and good facilities, a
good staff can work wonders. Congeniality is relatively easy to define,
and it differs very little from the retail environment to the school library
media center environment. It might be characterized primarily by
promptness. A friendly appearance, polite speech and manners, tolerance, and acceptance of individual differences are positive attributes that
contribute to a congenial atmosphere. Knowledge and the ability to show
respect for the question and the questioner are important elements. Notice that all these characteristics apply equally to any customer of any
age and to any type of library. If a staff member also happens to like
and enjoy working with young adults, as most school employees would
at a minimum allege that they do, it cannot do anything but help.

Chelton contends that:

> Library staff expect to see adolescent users as irresponsible and "dif-
> ficult," and adolescents expect to see staff as unhelpful and control-
> ling (page 7).

My experience has been that most teachers and library staff members
really do like teens and enjoy working with them. That's why they have
chosen to work where they do. Teens are seen as being challenging, of
course; and experience, both personal and professional, demonstrates
that they can be irresponsible. But that doesn't mean that the adults who
work with them in schools are not ready to give them another chance,
or that library staff members cannot approach a service encounter with
them in an open, friendly, and supportive way.

In regard to the latter part of Chelton's statement, negative student
attitudes toward school library staff is likely to be a given in the sense
that most students will profess, under certain circumstances, to hating
school and anything associated with school. However, given other circumstances, many students, perhaps even a majority of students, will indicate that they regard the library staff as being friendly and helpful

Action Plan #4: Sample and Survey

Sample whether customers leaving the library media center do so as satisfied customers or as disgruntled ones. Specify a period of time (hours, days, weeks) to collect data and select a method that will work best for you. Virginia Walter's excellent *Output Measures and More: Planning and Evaluating Public Library Services for Young Adults,* provides a brief overview of important sampling considerations (1995: 30). One might choose to keep a tally of the number of transactions that take place in and around the circulation desk. Most of these encounters will likely be routine. Most will likely be entirely positive. But it might be particularly interesting to take brief notes about any encounters with customers that seem to be negative. For example, criteria could be established such as that the customer expressed anger at or unhappiness with a staff member, that the customer felt the library's records were in error, or that the customer ran out of time, the copy machine didn't work, etc.

Examine the data:
What are the customer service implications? Additional investigation might explain the negative encounter: Is the customer unable to find the item they are looking for because it is not there? Perhaps the item can be reserved, obtained by interlibrary loan, or additional copies can be ordered. Or is it because they have overdue materials and policy prevents them from checking out more books until overdue items are returned? Maybe this policy is an important one in meeting the overall goals of the school or media center (teaching responsibility and consequences) and is important to continue to enforce without change. But if it is because the customer needed help and no one was available, perhaps there is a need for increased staff or for the reassignment of staff to different duties.

Communicate the data:
There are two recursive elements in the process of communicating data with the library staff. First, it is essential to effectively communicate the results of any information that has been gathered to all of the library staff. Depending on one's resources, this might be done by memo, e-mail, a staff meeting, posting the information in an accessible place, or a combination of these and other methods. Second, staff input about the interpretation and use of the data to improve customer service must be solicited and respected. It is, af-

---

Action Plan #4 (*cont.*)

ter all, the library staff that will be responsible for implementing any necessary changes. They are in the best position to recommend how they can work together to make the customer's library experience better. Every member of the staff will be empowered when they feel their input is welcome and considered, even if it is not used. And every effort should be made to see that it is used.

Use the data to change:
When the customer leaves the library feeling positive, who needs to be rewarded? Data obtained by exit survey can be used to make sure that the members of the library staff who are responsible for this positive customer service outcome see that their actions are noted and appreciated. If the customer's feeling is negative, the data can be used to illustrate to the staff members that a problem exists. They can collaborate to help determine a course of action to improve the situation next time.

The goal is to examine policies, procedures, attitudes, or other elements of the library that are amenable to change so that the customer, even if they are unable to be fully satisfied, leaves as often as possible with a positive feeling about the library and/or the interaction.

---

adults who can assist them in accomplishing things that they could not do otherwise. Students who have enjoyed years of positive experience in the children's departments of public libraries and in elementary library media centers have, by and large, a wealth of positive feelings about libraries on which secondary librarians can build. And in those situations in which a teen library customer is using a school library media center without a history of previous experience, they still are likely to come to the library with an expectation of getting help. Teachers will send them to the library with the suggestion that the facility exists and the staff is present for the express purpose of helping the student. Students tend to see the library as a place for them. (See Chapter Five, "Evaluating Customer Service," for results of a locally conducted library customer satisfaction poll.)

It's the moment of truth. If negative expectations are present on both sides, the question is whether or not each person, customer, and library service provider alike, can overcome those expectations to see and respond to each other as individuals. When the teen customer and the adult library service provider meet, it is the latter's responsibility, however, to ensure that the encounter is as positive as it can possibly be. Is it overly idealistic to believe that with the proper combination of library service zeal, interpersonal skill, content knowledge, and human caring that at least most of the time they can? If anyone's expectations are to change, let it be the teenager's perhaps negative, preconceived notions about librarians—make them see a positive, outgoing customer-centered side they might never have known existed!

SUPPORT STAFF EVALUATION AND STAFF DEVELOPMENT

Evaluation of the library media center support staff and staff development are not formally linked. They are distinct processes. Evaluation, at least in the formal, written sense, is likely the legal province of the building principal, and is probably formally described in the negotiated agreement under which they are hired. The library media specialist, however, may be asked to provide feedback to the principal about each employee's performance and may be encouraged to conference with each employee about their performance as part of this process.

The evaluation process can be stressful, especially when there are areas of concern or conflict that must be discussed. Some support staff members might be fearful of the entire process, fearing for their job. The primary emphasis should be that the evaluation process is for the purpose of reinforcing positive behaviors and valued skills; secondary considerations might include discussions of areas in need of improvement, or concerns about specific problems that must be addressed. The individual's strengths can provide a base from which to work on areas considered to be weak. For those areas that are in need of improvement, support can be provided, strategies for remediation can be negotiated, outcomes can be specified, and results can be monitored over time with the emphasis always firmly placed on using the process to make a good employee better.

Informal evaluation goes on all the time. As a consequence of working together in close quarters under what can, at times, be stressful conditions, the school library media specialist will often hear quite clearly and directly what the staff thinks or feels about library operation, issues, policies, and procedures. One cannot help but be cognizant of how work is being done by the staff. The tenor of interactions between staff members and customers, between staff members and each other, and between

Action Plan #5: Training

Library staff, student assistants, and/or other volunteers must be trained to provide excellent customer service. The librarian is in the best position to plan, deliver, and evaluate this training. Consider how and when such training might best be provided.

Staff will be most amenable to training when they are paid for their time. In schools this likely means such training must take place "on-the-job" as students and other library customers present themselves with "real world" needs. Teaching and learning has a pay-off for both the customer and library staff member in that the student's needs are met as the service is provided and simultaneously the staff member gains experience and knowledge. There are disadvantages, however, in that teaching and learning can be time consuming, so the customer must be able and willing to endure the extra time required to meet their need for service. Also, the teaching/learning encounter is likely to be quite public, so the level of trust and/or respect between the trainer/librarian and the learner/support staff member must be sufficient to allow for some risk-taking.

Informal, ongoing training-as-needed is probably the norm in most school library media centers. Presentation and discussion of any theory or philosophy of customer service principles are likely rare. Opportunities for practice such as via role-playing or other simulation are limited to brief moments of relative quiet or perhaps before- and after-school sessions. Consider how the essential elements of excellent customer service are communicated to the support staff. Role modeling is of prime importance. The librarian's behavior sets the norm and the standard for other employees. The librarian should include the library's customer service policies as part of the library's policy manual. This manual should be shared with staff to establish a base for discussion, training, and evaluation. A statement about the kinds of interventions to be used or additional training opportunities to be offered to staff in the event of less-than-satisfactory performance could be included. Consequences for continued failure to adhere to recommended customer service principles and guidelines should be made clear. Evaluation must include both a determination of the behaviors and practice currently observed and of what the librarian/evaluator would *like* to see being done.

Customer service itself must also be evaluated. Such evaluation might include an investigation into the service provided to one customer group over time ("What percentage of seventh grade students can use the catalog independently to locate materials for a project?" or "What percentage of faculty order videotapes from the Area Education Agency using the online reservations system?"). Another approach would be to examine one particular aspect of customer service, such as reference or circulation desk behavior or the number of computer users who did (or did not) experience a crash over a given period of time. Alternatively, one might find it useful to get a "snapshot" of customer service to all groups at one point in time.

staff members and other members of the school community affect the mood of the library and often are easily discerned. The media specialist sometimes receives feedback from students, teachers, and other school employees about the performance of the library staff. Praise for particularly noteworthy contributions above and beyond the normal call of duty is always welcome, but so must be complaints about a problem or comments about a conflict that may have occurred. As the library staff's direct supervisor, the librarian may be asked to intervene. It is amazing how complex some of these situations quickly become. A student, his or her parent/guardian, a teacher, or an associate or two can all be involved in some relatively simple situation like a student who seems not to have been where he/she was supposed to have been when he/she was supposed to have been there. The school's principal, counselor, or other school staff may sometimes be required to step in and help resolve the issue. On occasion, a parent must be called or a letter may be written home to detail a particular situation and explain the consequences for the student. It is important to ensure that all such communications follow building and district guidelines so that the library and its policies can and will be supported by the principal and district administrators if further action is necessary.

But if evaluation and staff development are not formally or directly linked, they may still be thought of as related. Both work better as ongoing relationships rather than as one-time events. A supportive relationship between the library media specialist and each library staff member in an atmosphere of mutual respect and trust can foster a give-and-take in which problems really are seen as opportunities to improve service (see Chapter 5, "Evaluating Customer Service"). When a difficult process, procedure, personal conflict, or disruptive incident takes place, talking together as a staff helps each individual see it from new angles. Examining the situation from the customer's point of view as well as one's own, for example, can help one be more sensitive to the customer's needs. Collaborative problem solving can be a key element in learning to work together as a team. Recognizing that each person's opinions are valuable, acknowledging that each person's contributions are necessary, and learning by experience that each staff member at least occasionally makes "mistakes" helps to improve staff attitudes and performance.

Good staff development provides employees with the necessary skills to improve their performance. It educates and informs, strengthens and enhances the employee's ability to do their job. The time available for formal staff development in schools for support staff tends to be very limited. A few hours or at most a few days of inservice each year may be directed specifically at media secretaries and associates. Unfortunately, it may be this "top-down," directed nature of the inservice opportunities that leads to a negative staff attitude about such training. Some associates choose to take a cut in pay rather than attend these staff development sessions provided. Too often they feel that they have little input about the content of these sessions and don't find them valuable. The institution can offer the opportunity, but beyond that? It's difficult to meet every individual's need for relevance.

That's another reason why informal, ongoing self-evaluation is a regular part of the routine for the librarian and library support staff members. The group is small and talk often turns to discussions about what works well with particular customers, situations, and circumstances. It's important for the staff to be aware that there is a fine line between such talk that is appropriate, professional, and positive versus chatter that devolves into negativity or gossip. Gossip has no place in the library; but library staff members often raise questions about particular incidents they encountered. They describe what happened and ask whether they did the right thing in that situation. Informal discussions almost always result in the staff member feeling they did the right thing, or the best they could under the circumstances. The greater the feeling of empowerment the staff feels to make decisions in their areas of responsibility, the less time the librarian must invest in such activity.

Opportunities for the library staff to get together for snacks or lunch (perhaps every Friday for example) to recapitulate the week's trials and tribulations can be helpful. Giving staff a chance to visit informally and talk about issues other than the day-to-day operation of the library can help people feel better about working together. At the same time such gatherings can provide opportunities for mutual support, strengthen relationships, and help keep everyone on the same page concerning procedures, operations, and management of the library. A side benefit is that this process reinforces the idea that students can and should learn from each other, even during informal situations in the library, because the staff regularly experiences that same relaxed learning environment.

ROLES: WE ARE HERE TO HELP

Teenagers often are reluctant to ask for help. Nothing is as frustrating as seeing a student about to leave the library media center empty-handed and asking, "Did you find what you were looking for?" only to be told, "No, I was looking for a book but couldn't find it." Almost universally, further questioning will show that at *no time* did the student ever approach a staff member to get help in finding the aforementioned book. The student simply walked in, looked around (with or without using the computer catalog), and was on the way out without ever having asked any staff member, several of whom may have been in plain sight, for assistance! Incredible. There are small signs taped at intervals on the shelves around the library that say, "If you don't find the book you are looking for, please ask any staff member for help." An orientation is provided to all incoming seventh grade students in which we introduce the library staff and explicitly ask students to search us out if they need help. The staff is hired, trained, encouraged, and rewarded for being friendly, open, and approachable. All library staff desks are out in the open so that students can see and approach staff at any time help is needed. Staff is urged to try to make contact with any student that looks as if he/she needs help. In fact, that's what I'm doing when I ask as they leave whether or not they've found what they were looking for. Clearly, there are some deeply ingrained teen/adult issues at work here. While we can't rewire the teen brain, we can be vigilant and provide staff intervention as often as possible.

Frequently, a little on-the-spot follow-up will locate the book the student wanted. It might be on the shelf where he/she should have been able to find it, or sometimes it is off somewhere, in a special display or perhaps on the cart to be reshelved. It always feels good to hand the book to the student with a flourish, knowing that this customer who was about to leave dissatisfied leaves happy instead. But the encounter is tinged with sadness, too, that the student did not have the wherewithal to have found it unassisted or to ask for help. It's a signal that we've failed to deliver optimal library customer service, which includes teaching customers sufficient intellectual and physical access skills so that they can locate materials independently. Increasing the amount of time spent teaching students to use the catalog and providing more formal practice of physical location skills is part of an ongoing effort to improve service in this area.

But remember, too, that students come to the library media center for reasons which range from the sublime (because of what we know, because of what we have, because of who we are) to the ridiculous (they want to wander the hall, they want a drink of water on the way to and from the library, they want to meet their beloved somewhere along the way, etc.). By providing excellent, congenial, prompt service to our customers, the library staff stands to make a long-lasting and positive impression, what we call "good feelings." If, as educators, we can nudge them along the path we intend so that the student also learns new skills, acquires a great book to read, or accomplishes some other new learning, that almost seems like gravy.

Yes, it is certainly true that many adolescents assume that any adult they see in the school library media center is the librarian. This is a variation of the fact that students, especially in elementary school, have no reason to differentiate between adults in their classroom. Whether the person is a volunteer, principal, student teacher, practicum student, psychologist, social worker, or other visitor, they are adults and need to be related to as adults. They are authority figures. In a pinch, any one of them may be approached with a request for information or to go to the bathroom. This assumption of adult authority is a mental shortcut, a generalization that lets the student deal with all these people in one fell

---

... service is a large part (32%) of what the librarian is doing, and an even larger part of what the library clerk is doing (49%) ... (page 169).

It is long past time that standards of practice and research studies took specific notice of the clerical presence in most libraries, instead of subsuming or ignoring it under discussions about policies. ... For many adolescents, the adult clerk whom they first meet at the circulation desk is the institutional representative of the library and its policies (page 202).

This [blurring of the roles between "professional" and "clerical" labor categories] may be why so many users think anyone who works in a library is the librarian (page 205).

Library practitioners would do well to note that users remember more how they are treated in a service encounter than what they get from it (page 206).

swoop—they are, in effect, teachers. It seems natural that this attitude carries over into the library, and carries into the teen years.

Salespeople and other guests to the library have to deal with the same ambiguity when several adults are present simultaneously. Gender stereotyping also comes into play, in that most visitors assume that the librarian will be female. In a library with female support staff and a male librarian, visitors almost always approach the female support staff person first, ignoring the male in the room. Nametags worn by all staff members can help if they are easy to read and provide both the person's name and position or assignment. Nametags imply some authority or legitimacy, and are considered in some schools to be a part of the safety plan, in that any person without a nametag should be approached by staff and directed to the office for identification.

But certainly another reason for role ambiguity is that many people simply have little idea of what distinguishes a librarian from any other living, breathing human being who works in the library. They don't know the professional training that librarianship requires, don't understand the jobs that librarianship entails, and don't have a very clear picture of how the librarian fits into the larger scheme of the school as a whole.

TALK THE TALK

It cannot be overemphasized how important it is to be precise and personable in conversations with our young adult library customers. These moments of truth are critical encounters that can have significant consequences for the customer and his/her relationship to the library. Therefore, the use of specific language is modeled for staff during training. Role playing allows staff to practice these strategies with each other in a supportive, low-threat environment. When working at the desk, staff members are encouraged to use the model language until it becomes second nature and they can improvise or adapt it based on their own personal style. They are instructed to ask, for example, as a customer approaches the desk with a book, "Would you like to check that out?" If an affirmative response is received, they then ask, "What is your last name, please?" This is preferred to the hard-edged and demanding "Name!" that has sometimes been heard in the past. Polite, softer language can make a real difference in how the customer feels. This simple act of kindness, this consideration, does much to impart the feeling that should characterize every library encounter. Staff then confirms that the correct customer's name is on the screen by further prompting, "And are you (first name)?" instead of demanding, "First name!" or even "First

Figure 3–1: LMC Student Assistant Orientation and Training Checklist

General
Behavior
Meet and greet
Send them out with something friendly
Use "please" and "thank you" whenever it's appropriate. Be polite, respectful, and professional.
Confidentiality of student records.

Appearance
Dress can be casual/normal school style, but should be clean.
Same goes for personal hygiene of hands, hair, etc.
Wash your hands frequently, including after checking in or otherwise handling lots of books. They tend to be dirty and dusty!

Computer
What should you do if the computer asks for a password? (Ask for help from LMC staff.)
What should you do if the book won't scan? (Enter the number from the keyboard.)
What does the beep mean? (The computer did something—look to see what it did!)
What if the barcode (displayed on the screen) does not match the book? Ask for help!

Daily tasks that can be done right away or as time allows:
Line up tables. Push in and straighten chairs.
Check encyclopedias to see that they are all there and in order. Indexes can stay flat on the shelf at the end of the set.
In the hall, your nametag is your pass. Wear it and do not disturb classes while going about your job.

Checking Books Out:
Check out books only in the name of the person who is standing in front of you.
Check out books in the name of a teacher only if the student has a note specifically making that request.
Move books from left to right as you check books out.
Look at the book to see if it needs repairs. We do not like to check out damaged books. If in doubt, ask one of the LMC staff to look at it with you and decide what to do.

You say, "Would you like to check out that book?
What is your last name, please?
"Can you spell that for me?" Or "How do you spell that?"

As you have this conversation, reach for the book(s) and put them beside the keyboard.

Enter the student's last name. Usually the first four or five letters is sufficient. Press "Enter".

Read the list of names to see if there is more than one person with the same last name. Scroll up or down using the arrow keys if necessary to find the right name. Or, if you are in the wrong part of the list, press "Esc" and start over.

Confirm that you have the right person by asking for their first name unless you absolutely know it for sure!

When you have the name of the person highlighted, press "Enter".

Their name should appear in the upper-right hand corner of the screen.

Under their name any books they have checked out will appear.

Be sure to note any information on the right, especially about overdues.

> **Any overdue books will highlight the date due.**
>
> **Students may not check out any books if they have anything overdue!**
>
> **If the student has an overdue, tell them what it is and ask them if they know where it is. Can they return it now? Can they return it today? Can they return it tomorrow?**
>
> **Keep the book and put it on the cart to be reshelved by staff. Do not give it back to the student!**

Also look for any other "unusual" markings on the screen, for example:

> "**R**" means there is a reserve on that item. Follow instructions below.
>
> "**M**" means there is a message on that item or patron. Ask LMC staff for help.
>
> Sometimes a red box or other message will appear. For example, it might say "Lost for 1 inventory period" or "Lost—paid for"

Scan the barcode of the book (or other material) using the handheld scanner.

When it beeps, read the screen to confirm that the proper information is displayed on the left.

Scan "check out". It should beep again. Confirm on the screen that the due date is displayed.

Stamp the date due slip with the date stamp. It should match the date on screen.

Hand book(s) to customer with a smile, thanks, or some kind of friendly send off such as "Enjoy the book" or "See ya later."

Can a student check out a book if they have something overdue? **(No.)**

Figure 3–1: (*Continued*)

Checking Books In:
Move books from right to left as you check books in.
Look at the book to see if it needs repair. If a book has been damaged by
the user, they are responsible for paying for the necessary repair or replacement. If you are in doubt about the damage you see (that is, whether
or not it is beyond normal wear and tear), ask one of the LMC staff to
look at it with you and decide what to do.

Scan in the book(s). Listen for the beep. Confirm that the correct info is
on the screen.
Scan "check in".
Look to see if there is any special note. For example,

1) if a name is listed under "Reserved", write the name on a yellow Post-
it note and put it inside the cover of the book sticking out the top.
**Do not write a date or anything else on the Post-it note un-
less you are specifically instructed to do so by the LMC staff.
(AM and PM "runners" will be told what else to do.)**
2) if the record says the book was checked out to "lost" or "lost-paid
for", please tell a member of the staff.

Put books on the cart to be shelved. Arrange in proper sections and put
them in order as time allows (F= Fiction, which are put in alphabetical
order by the author's last name, Dewey numbers=nonfiction, R= Reference, PB should be separated by genre and alphabetized by author's last
name, Pro=Professional, Kits and Videotapes go behind the circ desk—
ask for help!).
If checking in large numbers of books (such as carts coming in from classrooms) be sure to turn books down as they are done. Inform staff of
your ending point if you must leave before completing the job.

Renewing a Book:
(This is my favorite thing, 'cause it's so easy!)

Scan the book, scan renew. When it beeps, confirm that the correct info
(title, date, and patron name) are displayed.
Stamp the book with the due date and hand it to the customer with a
smile and goodbye.

If a student wants to renew a book that is overdue:
Check the book in.
Note the student's name.

Enter the student's name.

Check out the book.

Stamp the book with the due date and hand it to the customer with a smile and goodbye.

Reserving a Book:

When would a student put a book on reserve? (When there is no copy available to check out.)

How do you know there's no copy available for check out? (Look it up by title on the computer and make sure. Offer to help the student find the book if it IS available.)

To put a book on reserve:

Enter the student's last name. Proceed as if checking a book out to get the student's name on the screen.

Type in the title of the book. When the correct title is highlighted, press "Enter".

Scan "Reserve". Say "Yes" to the question in the red box, "Reserve all titles?".

Tell the customer that when the book comes in we will send them a notice. We will hold the book for them no more than two days after sending the notice. After that we give it to the next person on the list or put it out on the shelves.

To remove a student from the reserve list, enter the student's name, scan reserve, and highlight their name. Press "delete". OR enter the title, scan reserve, highlight the student's name, and press "delete".

Tour of the LMC:

"Our" work area and the students' work area.

Kits, videotapes, archived magazines, copy machine.

Computers and Lab II.

Reference

Story collections

Biography

Paperbacks

Nonfiction

Fiction

Professional

Books on tape

Current magazines

Newspapers

Production room and supplies.

Figure 3–1: (*Continued*)

Copy Machine:
Press "clear" button to restore default settings.
Standard copy. Line up original along left-hand edge and within the area marked in red.
> If the original is dark or has a dark edge or background, be sure it's against the left edge!

Press the green button.

Know how to
  1) Adjust lighter and darker
For each of the following, **ask for staff help:**
  2) Enlarge/reduce
  3) Two-sided copy, hand-fed
  4) Transparencies, hand-fed
  5) Load paper
  6) Clear paper jams
  7) Any other copy tasks

How to use the intercom:
Press the button and wait for the office to respond. Tell them what you need, such as, "This is the LMC. I need help." Talk back and forth, slowly and clearly, as needed.

The Phone:
If you hear a "beep" coming from one of our two phones, you may also hear someone ask for a staff member or deliver a short message such as, "Call for Joel on line 3." Answer them to let them know that the message has been received and then deliver the message to the appropriate person as soon as possible.

Fire and Storm Warning Alarms:
If the fire alarm goes off, proceed out the back door of the LMC, down the stairs, and across the drive onto the grass. Look for and stay near the LMC staff so we can account for your safety. Return to the LMC when the all-clear signal is given.

If the storm warning signal goes off, walk silently, single-file down the hall toward the computer lab along the right-hand side of the wall. Go down the stairs and into the wrestling room. Follow all instructions given by any teachers present, including taking cover if and when told to do so. Return to the LMC when the all-clear signal is given.

name, please?" The emphasis is on clarity, civility, and efficiency. (See Figure 3–1.)

For many student patrons, the student assistant or other staff member they encounter at the circulation desk is the only person they talk to when they come into the library. Except to get their pass signed by an adult when they leave, they may not have any contact with any of the adult library staff. Therefore, training of student assistants and library support staff emphasizes the importance of acting courteously and speaking clearly and respectfully to every patron. All staff members are reminded that without patrons there will be no job. They are told that it is their job to ensure that customers have a positive library experience. Staff is asked to remind students and other library customers that they should ask for help anytime it is needed. Questions answered in the short term pay great dividends in increased student learning over the long term.

As a book is being checked out, student assistants and staff alike are encouraged to talk with the customer. For example, the customer might be reminded of other books they have checked out if that can be done without sacrificing their privacy. If they have overdue materials the due date might be mentioned and a brief discussion about where the overdue material could be might ensue. The student is urged to make a verbal commitment to returning the overdue material as soon as possible so they can again check out library materials. No matter what the outcome of the transaction, staff is asked to say something like, "Thank you very much," "That is due _____," "Enjoy the book," or "See you later" as a closing to the encounter.

There is a huge difference in the response from students when a staff member approaches them in the stacks and says, "Hi. What can I help you with today?" instead of "May I help you?" The latter makes it too easy for the customer to say "No" which stops the encounter. The former informal and intentionally grammatically incorrect query, however, often invites an affirmative and fairly detailed response. It boils down to learning to avoid asking questions that can be answered with one word answers. To prompt customers, teen or otherwise, to talk, one should ask them open-ended questions that actually invite them to say something:

"Hi guys. What brings you here today?"

"Hello. I see you're looking at the (fill in the blank) books."

"Hi. Was that (fill in the blank) you checked out last week as good
as (fill in the blank)?"

"Hey, good to see you. What are you working on today?

Given a chance, most customers will be happy to have at least a brief
conversation, and sometimes it can quickly become meaningful. And that
conversation can help the librarian meet their informational needs
quickly and effectively. This is the positive kind of result librarians want
to achieve as often as possible from these small but important moments
of truth.

SUPERVISION

"Super-vision" as in Superman's X-ray eyes, would certainly be helpful
on occasion in spotting trouble before it goes too far in the school library media center. Actually, the wisdom of Solomon and the patience
of Job would come in handy, too. But the point is that when students
feel they can't be seen, they are more likely to do things (or at least try
to do things) that they shouldn't. Customer service includes doing everything possible to ensure that all library customers feel safe. Previous
mention was made (in Chapter 2) about the placement of a round, convex security mirror enabling staff to see areas of the room which would
otherwise be out of sight. Any instance of physical threat, bullying, or
taunting taking place in the library must be stopped immediately. This
strategically placed mirror combined with the fact that staff is asked to
be on their feet and aware of the customers who are in the room and
what they are doing at all times are two ways we attempt to provide the
kind of X-ray vision that can make the library the safe haven we want it
to be.

Another aspect of library supervision has to do with the creation of
separate work areas for different kinds of activities and varying levels of
noise. Mention was made earlier that at South East Junior High, the
desks of the associate, secretary, and librarian are in the most public part
of the facility, near the circulation desk and current periodical collections. These are certainly not always the quietest place in the library for
us to work, but it puts the service providers where the service is most
often needed. When it's quiet, staff can do quiet work. When it is not,
staff is busy with the bustle of library business.

A final aspect of supervision in which support staff play an important
role is in being aware of who is in the library and what they are doing.

We have had some incidents in which students were caught trying to steal books from our collection. Security cameras and electronic security systems to protect inventory are becoming ubiquitous in businesses as well as libraries, but they imply a lack of trust that some people find offensive. Inventories of the South East collection over the last decade indicate that losses could not begin to make a purchase of a $10,000+ security system cost effective. Most of the books lost to theft in a given year are paperbacks. Many of them are old enough that they have already depreciated significantly in value. Some of these lost books are eventually returned, often during the summer following the school year by a student's parent/guardian when a cache is found under a bed or in a backpack stuffed in a closet. Often there is a fairly substantial quantity of such stolen books found at one time. The value of hardback books stolen from our collection seldom exceeds a few hundred dollars per year Records indicate that in a bad year there may be about an equal dollar value lost in paperbacks, although most years it is only about half that amount. Any loss of books is heartbreaking and replacement of them can be difficult, time consuming, and/or impossible. Additionally, there are always a few books checked out to teachers in the building and via inter library loan to other schools that disappear. Again, the loss of any materials hurts, but at this relatively low level of loss these books can be replaced. Meanwhile the attitude of the library staff will be to watch our customers, but more with an eye to how they may be helped than because we suspect they are trying to rip us off.

REFERENCES

American Association of School Librarians and Association for Educational Communications and Technology. 1998. *Information Power: Building Partnerships for Learning.* Chicago: American Library Association and Washington, DC: Association for Educational Communications and Technology.

Chelton, Mary K. 1997. *Adult-Adolescent Service Encounters: The Library Context.* Ph.D. Dissertation. New Brunswick, NJ: Rutgers University.

Walter, Virginia A. 1995. *Output Measures and More: Planning and Evaluating Public Library Services for Young Adults.* Chicago: American Library Association.

Young Adult Library Services Association. 1993. *Directions for Library Service to Young Adults.* Second Edition. Chicago: American Library Association, 1993.

Chapter 4

Services to Students

Joel Shoemaker

LIBRARY POLICY AND LIBRARY CUSTOMERS: FREEDOM VS. CONTROL

Every school has a feeling about it, an emotional climate that many people report that they can sense when they enter, tour, and/or work in the building. It is logical to assume that the mood of a school and the mood of the library media center are likely to be in sync. The overall mood of the school influences how the students, faculty, and staff act, while simultaneously the ways they act do much to create and sustain the mood of the school. As the students behave in the school at large, one would expect them to behave in the library. The policies and rules that govern the life of the school affect how it is perceived by customers. While public schools do need to preserve and protect individual constitutional rights, their primary purpose has not been focused on maximizing individual freedom; indeed, they are more easily seen as institutions created for control. While different schools devise different schemes by which to exercise this control, managing large numbers of students in a safe environment involving a variety of staff members in a reasonably fixed schedule requires a fair amount of rigidity.

Most schools have a relatively high control factor. Students are supposed to be in class all the time unless they have a pass to be elsewhere. Students are not free to come and go from the school without permission from their parents and approval by the office. Students are not allowed to be in the building before a specified opening time or after a specified closing time without a pass from a teacher except in designated areas. Another example of control might be that during the school day passes to the library media center from study hall are limited to 15 (or 20 or 30) minutes unless a teacher gives them a pass for the entire period describing the student's purpose for being there. Thus, most students come and go within a short time and do not spend much time browsing or using the computers for exploration. The library may be open to students only a short time before school starts and for an hour or less at the end of the day.

In spite of such controls, many school libraries are active, happy places.

In contrast, a school library can look like a candidate for library heaven but be neither an active nor a happy place. Imagine a library with an outstanding collection of books. Every book by every popular author desired by the clientele is on the shelf, lined up, covered in clean, shiny protective covers, in an attractive, automated library. The reference collection is outstanding. The room is attractively furnished, clean, and comfortable. Unfortunately, the collection is pristine precisely because it is virtually unused. The students quite rightly perceive that they were not welcome. Those beautiful, plentiful books are not checked out, are not read, and are not used by students because the librarian is not a friendly, open, or welcoming person. She makes students feel unwelcome by her demeanor. She imposes severe restrictions on how many students may be in the library at one time, how long they may remain there, and how many books they may check out. She charges fines for overdues. She does not collaborate with her subject specialist teachers, so the curriculum does not include information literacy skills. If she is not the Wicked Witch of the East, she seems at least to have taken lessons from her. Again: if there is one vital difference between a happy library and an unhappy one it is in the library staff.

It is interesting, then, to examine existing library policies in terms of how they affect customer service. For example, consider that the following simple, straightforward, very typical library policies have both the positive consequences they were intended to have and that they might, simultaneously, have unintended, negative consequences as well.

Much of life in school boils down to a question of balance between freedom and control. Educators try to find the right point between absolute freedom on one hand and absolute control on the other that allows learning to take place in as efficient a manner as possible. In administering the library, one must seek the same balance. If the library policy allows customers to check out an unlimited number of materials, some students will handle this freedom responsibly and others will lose

Table 4.1

Policy	Purpose	Unintended consequence
Before students may use the Internet at school, both the student and his/her parents/guardians must sign an "acceptable use agreement" which specifies the conditions of use and consequences for misuse.	Students and their parents/guardians are advised about the Internet and our policies for its appropriate use for school projects; they know that students may lose access privileges if they break the rules.	Some students never get the permission slip signed and returned and so never learn to use this potentially valuable resource; some may be so afraid of making a mistake they avoid using the Internet as a resource; some have little time to use the Internet in class and have no study halls, so have little opportunity to use the resource; some break the rules and get away with it, and brag to other students that there is nothing wrong with doing what they are doing, undermining respect for the system.
Reference books may not be checked out by students.	To ensure that these expensive, large resources that are seldom read cover to cover are available at any time for any customer who needs them.	The student customer who needs and wants to use the reference material at home cannot do so, but instead must use it 1) only in the library, 2) in a teachers' room, or 3) by photocopying the most critical portions. Knowing they can't check reference books out, many students choose not to use them at all, preferring to spend their time looking for resources they can take home. Reference sources are thus underutilized.
Students who have overdue materials may not check out any additional materials until the overdue items are paid for or returned.	To reduce the number of lost books by not allowing students who have already shown themselves to be "irresponsible" to check out additional items.	Some students steal the additional books they want or need. Other students have a friend who has no overdues check out the desired item(s) for them. Consequently, an even greater number of books may actually disappear because they are stolen or lost. Interpersonal friction also sometimes develops over the books checked out by former "friends," etc.

Table 4.1 (cont.)

Policy	Purpose	Unintended consequence
Students who are not in class must have a pass saying where they are going and when they should arrive there.	To ensure that we can account for where students are and what they are doing at all times that they are at school. We also need to be able to find students when parents call and in the case of fire and/or storm alarms.	Students get the message that they can't be trusted, that they have no freedom to decide what they will do or when they will do it. They have little flexibility or freedom of movement within the school except in prescribed circumstances. (By the way, it's really not as bad as this sounds. Every student also gets twelve bathroom/locker passes each trimester to use more or less at their discretion. Many teachers similarly provide a virtually unlimited number of library passes that students can use almost any day.)

more books than they would if they were limited to a smaller number. If too many teachers check out a boombox to keep in their room to play music during their prep periods, there won't be one for the next teacher who comes in to get one for a teaching activity. If we allow students to use the video cameras and tripods without instruction, they will get broken more often. If we allow coaches to take the video cameras to sports events over the weekend, some of them will not be returned in time for use in class Monday morning.

What are the costs of institutional rules? Individual freedom can be denied or at least limited anytime that people are forced to act as members of a group. Individual behavior and therefore freedom of expression may be constrained in these situations. In looking for ways to assert their independence, to buck the system, to rebel against the strictures put in place to control the teaching/learning environment and make the institution work for the majority, individual students may act out in inappropriate ways. Others may look for things they can do to "get back at" the system. Some are made to feel that they are outsiders who don't fit in. In creating this place called school, policies are devised in the hopes that they will work for most people most of the time in most ways. Dealing with the unintended consequences by modifying the policies in response to individual needs is an ongoing process.

SPECIAL POPULATIONS MEAN SPECIAL OPPORTUNITIES FOR SERVICE

Serving the needs of our special education students presents some special challenges and opportunities in the library media center. Some of these have to do with the collection, others with the staff, and some with service.

The collection development difficulties spring from the fact that special needs students often want books and other instructional materials that look and feel like the ones used by regular education students their own age. Unfortunately, the so-called "hi-lo" (high interest, low vocabulary) materials and basic literacy materials available seldom cover the kind of content required by the secondary school curriculum at sufficiently low reading levels. Special education students who read at the primary level are likely to have few materials in the regular collection to choose from. Collaboration with special education teachers should be part of a concerted effort to strengthen this part of the school library's collection. But even the addition of several hundred titles that are at or below the fifth grade reading level, for example, do not begin to adequately cover every curricular area in a school's program of studies. They certainly cannot provide a satisfactorily varied menu of recreational reading options. And clearly they are not likely to be able to accommodate the needs of students who are nonreaders or read at the first or second grade level. This problem is not easily solved by requesting interlibrary loan materials from elementary collections because, again, those materials are written, edited, produced, marketed, selected, and purchased for younger readers. They seldom have the right look and feel for other students.

One aspect of our service to special education students has to do with the fact that some special education students look and behave in ways that are different than regular education students. They are "identifiable" and thus, to some students and library staff, they become somewhat scary or frightening. Some of this comes from a general discomfort with the unknown, or with what is unfamiliar. In addition, some of these students are louder than some other groups of students. Their vocalizations may sound like a scream or yell that are not appropriate in the library environment. At these times it is almost always the case that a special education associate is present and works to get the student to control vocalizations that are too intrusive for circumstances and, if necessary, return with the student to their classroom. Several of our current special education students cannot speak, although some do make sounds. When these individuals come to the circulation desk to check out books their difficulty (or inability) to communicate as effectively or completely as most regular education students sometimes translates into staff frustration or impatience. In nearly every case this frustration is masked so that it is not expressed to the student or other members of the library "public." But it is sometimes a cause for staff concern that has been expressed on numerous occasions after the students leave.

Some special education students do not use the library media center at all, at least in the traditional sense. Some are severely autistic, or are emotionally or socially unable to operate with the degree of independence required to use the library. Others are medically fragile and require the constant support of one or two associates just to maintain body functions. Because these students are "identifiable," when they do something negative the library staff is sometimes more likely to notice. When some special education students lose a book or return it in severely damaged condition, it can seem as if they are more irresponsible with the materials than other students. In the absence of real data, our discomfort (dare I say prejudice?) might make us act as if it were true. Thus, when a special education student comes to the circulation desk to check out materials, we might be tempted to say something like, "Now you've got to take care of this book—remember what happened last time . . . ?" The question is, would we, under the same circumstances, say the same thing to a regular education student who had similarly lost a book or returned one in damaged condition? I know that many of our special education teachers and support staff make extraordinary efforts to assist us in working with their students to ensure appropriate and responsible use of library materials. Similarly, it is an important part of our job to work with them to teach these identified special education students to the best of our ability. They are entitled by law to " . . . a free appropriate education" in which "'appropriate' means an education comparable to the education provided to nonhandicapped students. When identified, a handicapped student can expect that reasonable accommodations will be made so that the student receives an appropriate educational experience" (Grohe, Grieves, and Colman, n.d.).

Associates and student volunteers who accompany these students to the library media center do their best to provide almost continuous one-to-one supervision. Nevertheless, some students seem to "get away" and wander off on their own. My staff has been known to ask, in moments of pique, "What are they here for, anyway? What are they learning? All they are doing is making more work for me. I just put all those books away and now they're back in here messing them up. How are the regular education students who can actually use those books going to find the books they need if they are scattered all over the library?"

It is easy to get angry (or laugh) at this attitude. What are library employees hired to do but to work? What does it matter whether the work of putting books back and in order is necessitated by the activities of a special education class or a science class doing a research project?

The answer is that special education students are most certainly our customers, too. Common sense, policy, and the law all support the fact that every one of these students needs and deserves the same access to our materials, service, and professional abilities as any other customer. So the question is not "What are they doing to us?" The question is, "What are we doing for them?" Furthermore, how can we best provide the services they need? And how can we do our part to ensure that they are included as respected members of our educational community?

The answer is that we do so by treating them the same way we do any other customer, only more so. We may have to be more patient, more polite, more certain to listen carefully. We have to use our hearts as well as our heads. We have to do our jobs as well as we can every moment every day, for every student, every teacher, every customer, day after week after month after year, year-in and year-out.

In the end, of course, every student, every customer, is a special population of one, each individual customer must be treated with equal respect, care, and attention if the best possible customer service is to be provided. Each reader's unique needs, desires, and tastes must be considered in providing excellent readers' advisory service. Each researcher's unique information needs, learning style, and time available for the task must be considered to provide excellent reference service. Each individual teacher's needs for materials, equipment, and technical support must be based on their knowledge, teaching style, time available, etc. Each request is unique. The number of special needs we meet is equal to the number of customers we see.

The parent who calls up to talk about what kind of computer to buy for their child; the associate who asks for help in using the World Wide Web to find out about becoming a naturalized citizen; the administrator from downtown who calls to ask for a book to read aloud during a special event; the home-schooled child who needs an account on the server to store his electronic portfolio; the kitchen staff member who calls to ask for help with her e-mail account; the "temp" hired to transcribe classes for a hearing impaired student who needs help printing from her laptop; the principal who can't get her new piece of equipment to work; the secretary whose computer keeps freezing—each has a special need. Each requires special attention. Each represents a special population of one and is a customer who can leave the encounter with the library media staff with a feeling of satisfaction or of displeasure.

TRANSIENCE

The student population today is increasingly mobile. Compared to some schools in other parts of the country, the rate of student turnover at South East Junior High must be laughably low. But these transient students are another identifiable special population who could benefit from a certain degree of special library media service. As new students arrive they need instruction about how to use the resources and services of the library media center. Until researching to write this book, I had no firm idea just what a significant portion of our total population these new students represent. The counselor's secretary was able to quickly generate a report on her automated student records program that tells how many students have left our school and how many have enrolled. Maybe you can get the same information for your school. Depending on the answer you get, you might find that, like me, it is time to do more for this group of customers.

During the first eight months of the 1999–2000 school year, 78 students enrolled and 79 students withdrew from a student population of about 800 students. This meant that 10 percent of the students who spent some time learning how to use our collection and tools were gone, and ten percent of the students who were currently enrolled had no formal introduction to the library, library staff, collections, electronic tools, network, policies, or procedures. Can either you or I afford to assume that ten percent of our customers will pick up what they need to know about our library on their own?

In almost all secondary schools, students who are enrolled at the beginning of the school year are provided with a short, basic orientation to the library through tours the library media specialist conducts for at least the incoming class of students. Additional instruction is provided in the use of specific tools such as the catalog, periodical indexes, and the Internet through whole-class assignments and projects, usually during the first few months of school. But students who enroll after this instruction has been provided may receive no formal orientation program or instruction. They are often expected to learn what they need to know independently. Students are sometimes paired with mentors, students in their classes, who help them as needed. And both teachers and the library staff work with students individually as time and opportunity allow to answer specific questions. But it is a simple and obvious fact that customer service to this segment of the student population could be and should be significantly improved. Like some other aspects of good library customer service, this need seems so obvious that it must be a common part of library school education, and an orientation process for new students may be common practice in many school libraries around the country. But it may be the kind of thing that you, like me, have just let slide . . . until now.

What if, as a matter of course, every newly enrolled student was provided with a "library media center orientation packet" that included a map of the library media center, a handout with the pictures of each library staff member, their names, and a description of the services they provide? Such a packet would have been difficult to produce in the past, but with today's computer graphics programs and laser printers, it is much easier. It could include a coupon good for one (or one thousand!) "free checkout(s)," a bookmark, or perhaps a short, self-guided, self-scoring tour of the facility (exercises that students would complete and "grade" independently, with library staff available for assistance if needed). Another coupon could offer a "free" lesson in using the Internet or the computer catalog to find information on any topic of their choice.

Using the coupons would allow library staff to keep a record of which new students had taken advantage of this opportunity. Additional follow-up would be that much easier if it were deemed necessary.

The idea would be to provide just enough information in the packet to make the student feel comfortable coming in to use the library without overwhelming them with too much detail. Ideally, the information would be presented in an informal, entertaining way. The packet could be given to the student as part of their enrollment procedure in the counselors' office, or they could be introduced to the library staff and given the packet at the library circulation desk after completing registration. Although the primary purpose of the packet would be to provide the student with a positive, helpful, and supportive introduction to the library media center, it could also be a very positive public relations tool when shared with the student's parent/guardian, and might even prove to be a useful handout for other library visitors, too.

Some new students will have little or no previous experience using computers. Understandably, they tend to be a bit stressed out when confronted with a computerized catalog, a large number of computer-based applications, tools, and processes, especially if they have never had keyboarding instruction. The library media center computers might include a self-paced keyboarding instruction program. This could be used by any student for practice at any time, but would be especially useful for these new, inexperienced computer users.

This orientation packet need not be a "paper and ink" production, but could be mounted as part of the library media center homepage, accessible to anyone from any computer at any time. New students could be shown how to access the packet, how to print all of it or only the parts they need, and be well on their way to independent and confident use of the computers as they gain the information they need to succeed in using the library.

The bottom line? Customer service to students in school library media centers means considering each student as an individual, while also looking for opportunities to meet the special needs of identifiable groups of students. The highest level of customer service always involves a melding of the interactions between a kind, humane, and knowledgeable library staff with unfettered customer access to the best available resources.

REFERENCE

Grohe, Barbara, Tim Grieves, and Marian Colman. n.d. *Section 504 Plan and Compliance Procedures*. Iowa City Community School District.

Chapter 5

Evaluating Customer Service

Joel Shoemaker

One ought to consider the antithesis to library heaven: what must library hell be like? I don't even want to think about it. All the materials, such as they are, are housed there within the walls. The collection, whether inadequate, musty, and outdated or shiny, new, and in perfect order, sits untouched and useless on the shelves. Ranks of record players, filmstrip projectors, and maybe a reel-to-reel tape recorder or two sit, dust-covered, along slightly sagging storage shelves. Library hell is a quiet place. There are no customers.

People, however, can be seen to inhabit the place. The librarian and her assistant lurk behind their desks, pencils jabbed in their severely tied buns, guarding the entrance with their steely gaze lest anyone should think of coming in to request service or information. When provoked to speak, the librarian's voice is oily smooth, but one senses somehow that every question is a trap, every encounter runs a risk of permanent and perhaps fatal injuries of the spirit. There is sharpness here. There is danger and a feeling of unreality. "Abandon hope all ye who enter" might well be carved over the door. One can never hope to see one's way through the gloom and dank atmosphere of the place to find anything worthwhile. There is no way one can tell the librarian about one's heart's desire. No person could withstand her glare, her withering glance, and her slack-eyed dismissal. "Is it knowledge you seek, miscreant? Begone! Darken my door no more—I'm maintaining the computer catalog."

How does one tell whether their library or media center is closer to library heaven or library hell? Aside from checking to see if there is a pencil stuck in your hair, you might want to try questionnaires, surveys, and other time-tested means of assessing the quality of the services you and your library provide.

RISKS AND REVELATIONS: GOOD NEWS IS GREAT TO HEAR . . .

Direct feedback from students, teachers, and other customers is wonderful when it is positive. Isn't it marvelous when a student or other customer makes a point of stopping by to say that they really liked that last book you recommended? It can make your day when a teacher with whom you collaborated reports that they are thrilled with the positive results of the new unit of study you helped create. It feels great when a consultant or other outside speaker for whom you spent considerable time and energy setting up equipment for a presentation sends a note of thanks. Do not dismiss or denigrate the importance to one's self-image of any pleased and appreciative customer. It feels great to receive a heartfelt "thank you," and when a student or other customer takes the time to express their appreciation for the job you have done for them, it really makes your day. But if these ephemeral exchanges between customers and the librarian are the only form of feedback concerning customer satisfaction in the library, it may be difficult to prove one's worth to the faculty, principal, library system, or the district when budget cutting time rolls around. These expressions of appreciation feel great, but the fact is that the undocumented good one does in the library will not count when it comes to crunch time. It tends to be forgotten, glossed over, or ignored. It might as well have never happened. Aside from saying, "Would you mind repeating that for my principal?" or "Could you put that in my personnel file?" what's a librarian to do?

. . . BUT SOMETIMES THE NEWS IS BAD

It's difficult to spend much time in the retail environment without encountering an opportunity to provide feedback about the quality of the service or products. Although retail has taken a public relations hit over the last several decades in terms of how customer service is provided, many businesses are striving to improve. One is frequently asked, "Is there anything else I can get for your today?" Whether one is at the lumberyard, a pizza place, a local hospital, or a flower shop, on the table or near the cash register, there will probably be a short survey or response card that asks a few questions about the quality of your experience, the food, service, or physical environment. It may be comprised of a post-age-paid postcard that invites open-ended responses or comments about the quality of your shopping experience. It may be a short list of areas for you to rate on a scale from poor to excellent. It may probe your opinion about a particular aspect of the business that is a current focus for the company. In whatever form it takes, it implies, at least, that the company respects the customer enough to value the customer's opinion. And one assumes that the comments the customer makes will be read, tabulated, considered, and in all probability responded to in some way. While the business takes a risk in that they might get complaints instead of praise, it is an effective method to see how services are being perceived.

The secret to continuous improvement is to avoid becoming defensive, trivializing, or ignoring complaints as if they have no merit. It sounds like a cliché, but the fact is that every complaint is an opportunity to learn something, to change something so that it will work better next time. An excellent report is available online called, "Serving the American Public: Best Practices in Resolving Customer Complaints" (National Performance Review, 2000). The most basic idea is that the easier it is for customers to tell you their complaints, the easier it will be for you to resolve them. Another main point is that one should attempt to resolve complaints quickly and with the fewest possible intermediaries. If the service provider, for example, a library associate, can be empowered to resolve a complaint about a lost book directly and without assistance, the customer and the associate both are likely to be happier than if they must refer the problem to the librarian for resolution. This saves both time and money. A third point is that computers should be used to create a database of complaints so that over time, trends can be analyzed. This information should be made available to everyone in the business, from the support staff to the principal or library director, so that everyone can contribute to solutions.

Librarians have traditionally not felt much need to engage in this type of information gathering. In fact, an e-mail survey posted to an automated list for K–12 Iowa library media specialists asked, "How do you know if you're providing good customer service in your school library media center?" Among the first responses was:

> I don't think too many school librarians put too much emphasis on evaluating the level of customer satisfaction. It's one of those things that sounds logical when you hear about it in graduate school; it's one of those things you might read about in a book or journal article; but it's also one of those things that your principal will not

likely ask you about. It is not likely to be part of the evaluation instrument used to determine whether or not you keep your job. It's completely off the radar screen of any of the students, staff, or others who use your facility—they just want to get a good book to read or find out what they want to find out. So it becomes a low priority for the librarian (read, it doesn't get done). This is really too bad because I think most of the time it would provide the librarian with positive feedback that would not only make him/her sleep better at night, but also could be used in negotiations with the principal for increased funds, staff, services, and other kinds of needed support.

A sampling of other respondents' opinions:

- If no one is complaining, one must be doing a pretty good job.
- I have repeat customers who seek me out for specific help, recommendations for books to read, demonstrate that they have learned to locate information by themselves and the like.
- I am busy, so I must be doing something right.
- I help them find what they need and do not turn them away empty-handed.
- Patrons leave smiling.
- Staff members' opinions can be solicited as part of the evaluation process following joint curricular projects. In addition to a discussion about the relative success of the unit, the evaluation of the student learning and the projects themselves, the library media specialist can solicit input about the library collection, the tools used, and their level of satisfaction with the performance of the library staff and the library facility. Again, this information can be useful when talking with the school principal or district administrators about the need to upgrade the budget, facilities, staff, and the collection.
- There is no other place for the students and teachers to go for the materials and services they need.

"There is no other place for [them] to go. . . ." What a chilling thought. If the customers only come to the library because they have no other place to go, it is an indictment. In this day and age, most library customers have a plethora of other places they can go, starting with bookstores and the Internet for information and entertainment, and multiplying from there through an extensive list of activities and leisure-time options that make the library relatively expendable—unless it gives them good reasons, usually service-based, people-centered reasons, to continue to frequent the place.

Think of the school cafeteria as a parallel example: Is it the only place to go for food today? If the cafeteria workers prepare every food item in such a way that it becomes an unpalatable mush which is slapped onto trays with disdain, customers will vote with their lunchbags and sales will fall. Open campuses will see more and more students departing to take advantage of nearby food service options.

Recall a typical visit to a fast food restaurant. Did the clerk at the counter greet you? (Yes.) How were you greeted? (Politely; perhaps with a smile while the clerk asked, "May I help you?" or "Hello, what can I get you?") When your order was complete, what did the clerk do? (Looked you in the eye and asked if you'd like to super-size that or asked if that would be all. Then they repeated your order to check for accuracy, accepted your money, returned your change, and went to get your food.) When the order was complete, what did the clerk do? (Slid it toward you with a smile and delivered a closing message [perhaps while handing you your change] such as "Enjoy your meal" or "Have a nice day.")

Is there any reason that customers in the library should be treated with any less consideration than they are at the local hamburger joint? Consider the improvement in perceived customer satisfaction if every teenager who checked something out of the library received service that paralleled this typical fast food exchange. Clearly, it could do nothing but help.

And what if the library surveyed exiting customers the way a fast food restaurant does? A small survey could be distributed to each customer at the circulation desk as they are checked through. It could be formatted as a bookmark. Different colors of paper could be used each week or month (or day shift versus night shift) to make it easier to track trends over time. It could pose a few simple questions, such as:

1) Did you find what you were looking for today?
   Yes   No
2) Did you need help from the library staff today?
   Yes   No
3) Did you get the help you needed?
   Yes   No
4) Were you happy with the way you were treated by the library staff?
   Yes   No
5) Let us know what we could do to make the library better . . .

Please return this survey with the book or drop it in the box in the office, the lunch line, or in your reading or language arts class.

A SIMPLE SOUTH EAST SURVEY

In May 2000, six language arts classes were surveyed about the quality of library service at South East Junior High. The survey queried 144 seventh and eighth grade students (about 20 percent of the total population). The culminating question was, "Overall, how satisfied are you with the service you get in the library?" The five foils, listed in the table below with the number and percent of each response indicated, show an overwhelmingly positive response. But without some baseline to compare them to it's probably wise to hold off on any celebrating.

N=144 (19% of 750 students)	Very Satisfied	Mostly Satisfied	Satisfied	Not Very Satisfied	Not Satisfied at All
Number (Percent)	59 (41%)	49 (34%)	29 (20%)	7 (5%)	0 (0%)

The total number of students indicating that they were satisfied or better was 137 (95 percent) while only seven (5 percent) were not satisfied.

Also of interest are their written comments. The compliments are a great morale booster. It is interesting to see that essentially the same answer frequently showed up in each of the three "positive" columns, for example:

"Whenever I come in here there is someone to help me. Answer a question, recomend (sic) a book, etc." was from a "Very Satisfied" customer.

"I don't come very often, but when I do come the staff is very useful at helping me to find and check out what I need" and "Everything was fine and I got help if I needed it" were merely "Satisfied" customers.

A selection of other positive comments:

"I am satisfied because they can help me with a lot of things like find a book, look up something, etc. They are very nice too. They always help you find something."

"The help is superb. And it's a nice place to be. Nothing like the dark dismal elementary school libraries."

"This is one of the best school libraries I have been in. The people actually want you to check out a book! It also has an excellent selection."

"Very satisfied because the liberians (sic) come up to you when your (sic) there for awhile and ask you want (sic) book your (sic) interested in, and they find you a book."

But balance those positive comments with these:

"Sometimes when I go to the library people are really helpful, but most of the time I have to stand there and wait for help. The staff could try to do a little better at helping students."

"Sometimes the service is not good, and anoying (sic) staff is way to (sic) eager to help and that becomes anoying (sic)."

"When I check out a book their (sic) always making mistake (sic) and saying that I have overdue books when I really don't that's why I'm not very satisfied."

"[I marked 'Not Very Satisfied'] Because you (sic) limited time and the help doesn't is (sic) sometimes mean."

Other less-than-satisfied respondents said there was not always someone at the circulation desk to check out books when they were ready to go, and another said that some books were missing from certain series.

Sophisticated surveys would produce more sophisticated results, but this simple survey produced an interesting and useful range of forthright comments about both what we were doing right last year in the library and ways the library can improve. A more thorough analysis of these survey results will be shared with the entire library staff in the fall so that goals can be set for improvement. A follow-up survey will be conducted the following spring. The library staff is aware that customer service issues have high priority. These survey results are one way targets can be set so that the entire staff can work together to find ways to make the library media center work better for all our customers. For more information and another sample poll, see *Output Measures and More: Plan-*

Action Plan #6: Survey Your Customers

Would you be reluctant to provide a questionnaire or conduct a survey for fear of what the customers might say? Or are you pretty confident that so many of the answers would be positive that you would not learn anything useful? Does the idea of surveying your customers seem like an idea that is fine in theory but that you are just too busy to do right now? Have you thought of doing something like this before but decided to wait a little while, " . . . until things aren't so busy"?

Now is your time!

Take the chance, take the time, and try it. The results don't have to be made public if they are terrible! But they will establish a baseline from which you and your staff can work to improve. And the results might surprise you. They will likely be pretty positive, overall, and will tell you many things you are doing that customers already appreciate. Maybe there will even be some testimonials or other results that could be placed in your personnel file for the principal or director to consider along with other factors at evaluation time. If information is power, if information is good, if information leads to knowledge and understanding, then the more information you can gather, the better.

Start with something simple. Ask every customer who comes in your library tomorrow, "Did you find what you were looking for?" Record the results and share them with your staff. Discuss the results. What might they mean? Use what you learned to make a change or two. Live with those changes for a time and survey your customers again in the same way. Make such inquiries a normal part of doing business. Doing so will help send a message to your customers that you are aware of their needs and striving to meet those needs. It will mark you as a person who is interested in improving the library and the services it provides. It will establish you and the library as a proactive, results-based part of the institution.

---

ning and Evaluating Public Library Services for Young Adults (Walter, 1995: 61–65). An additional sample survey of young adult library customers is provided in *Connecting Young Adults and Libraries* by Jones (1998: 26).

And one last positive comparison to the retail world: at the cash register of a department store one is told, "Thank you for shopping with us today. Have a great day." Make your library customers feel at least as well about their library by ensuring that when they leave the circulation desk they receive a positive send-off such as, "Hope you enjoy the book!" or "Hey, let me know what you think of this one—I have not read it yet" or "Thanks for coming in!"

CONCLUSION

Frankly, I suspect that the biggest cause for poor customer service in libraries is that routine sets in. When behavior becomes too routine people get bored, and boredom kills individual attention. People get tired. They have bad days. Other things in their life take their attention sometimes and they forget to treat every customer with the same diligence, respect, and kindness that they might normally exhibit.

Demands for services can be overwhelming. Too many classes with too many customers with too many needs can place so many demands on a limited number of staff simultaneously that some needs will not be met, especially not to the high level of quality to which they aspire. Coping mechanisms vary. Study hall may need to be informed that no more students should be sent during that period. A group of students who just appeared from a class may need to be sent back with a note to the teacher explaining that they can't be helped just then. More likely, the entire library staff will simply redouble their efforts to work as quickly and efficiently as possible and to offer each customer in turn an apology for the delay in getting to them. The customers know they are part of a crowd, know the staff is working diligently, and generally are understanding. Flexibility really is the watchword. Teachers' contracts have for many years included a catchall clause that says something like, " . . . and other duties as assigned." This gives the principal the flexibility to deal with unexpected emergencies. Attending evening events like open house, back to school night, orientation meetings, etc., are covered by this blanket statement, but it also means that teachers grow to expect the unexpected. Librarians, who are teachers first and foremost, similarly grow used to being flexible in meeting the needs of their customers and in delivering the best possible service. Changing circumstances, less than ideal conditions, the daily wear and tear of the school environment may intrude, may inhibit one's efforts, but they must not be allowed to prevent the library staff from accomplishing their instructional or customer service goals for the students and other customers.

In terms of customer service, the goal is to treat each customer, each time, as if they are the first, the only, and the most important customer of the day. But when one repeats the same task, such as checking out materials, over and over again, hour after hour, day after day, and month after month, it is difficult to maintain the enthusiasm, freshness, and sincerity that one felt the hundredth, thousandth, or ten thousandth time the process is repeated. Whether the task is answering a reference question, showing a customer how to use the computer catalog, taking a customer to a particular book, or demonstrating how to use a piece of software, people get tired. In libraries, especially those with little or no support staff, one by necessity switches constantly from one job to another. Uninterrupted time is virtually unknown. This constant variety may allow one to stay relatively fresh at each one, at least until exhaustion sets in and one cannot put forth the necessary energy for any of the tasks at hand. Larger staff size allows for some specialization. Ironically, while this specialization allows one to develop expertise that should enhance customer service, allowing a higher level of service, it may simultaneously lead to boredom. One's voice is likely, over time, to betray a certain weariness or flatness. One's body language might suggest that one can barely stand to do this one more time. Or one might be genuinely displeased at being interrupted from some other, perhaps time-critical, task to help with this request. One might resent that this request for service is being made at all, believing that the customer should not need to ask this question. If/when this negative attitude is communicated to the customer, it cannot help retain that customer, build support for the library program, or improve the image of the library or library staff in that customer's eyes.

Routine is like a glacier. It wears one down so gradually one isn't aware of the change in the short term; but over time, or seen from a different vantage point, the change is clear. It stamps out individuality. It dampens creativity. It weakens sincerity. It makes it easy for the customer to perceive that they are merely a cog in some bigger wheel, that they are not cared for, respected, or important to the service provider or the library. It allows them to think that what they are or what they do does not matter. Anonymity is an enemy of the library that cares for its kids. Establishing relationships, communicating, sharing in a vital, holistic, learning environment in which the needs of each individual are equally and mutually respected is the goal. The middle school movement embraces concepts such as strengthened homeroom programs, school-within-a-school organizational schemes, and curricular teaming to promote the individuation of students in an effort to ensure that every individual feels a part of the main. The education profession did not need Columbine to prove that disaffected youth who feel left out, marginalized, or alienated are a matter of concern for the entire community. Bringing in the outsiders, finding ways to build bridges to them instead of erecting walls around them is critical. Some kids make it hard to do, but the library is an excellent place to make this happen. Librarians generally don't give grades so most students don't immediately perceive librarians as the enemy. Librarians generally don't give homework so librarians are not as likely to be seen as part of the evil empire. Librarians don't always make teen customers sit down and be quiet so librarians are not always thought to be controlling. And libraries are full of neat stuff like books, magazines, and computers—free!— that satisfy real needs and wants for the customers.

Libraries are for customers. Serve the customers well and they will continue to demand library service and support our efforts to provide that service. Libraries ignore their customers at their peril. The library that forgets their service role will fade away into irrelevance. Let boredom and routine lead to a feeling that the customers are being ignored and rancor will follow. Bottom line? The library is one of the best places for teens. It can be the best place, it ought to be the best place, and a focus on providing excellent customer service can make it the best place. The library can be the best expression of a community's commitment to its citizens to encourage an active, lifelong, inquiry-based model of learning that makes for a rich, fulfilling, and successful life. And it all revolves around those myriad moments of truth, when a customer and a librarian encounter each other and the quality of customer service hangs in the balance.

Let the balance tip in favor of the customer. Let your customers know that they are the reason you are there. Let the moment of truth be a victory for both the teen customer and for you, the entire staff, and the library.

REFERENCES

Jones, Patrick. 1998. *Connecting Young Adults and Libraries: A How-To-Do-It Manual.* Second edition. New York: Neal-Schuman.

National Performance Review. 2000. "Serving the American Public: Best Practices in Resolving Customer Complaints" [Online]. Available *www.npr.gov/library/papers/benchmark/bstprac.html* [July 3].

Walter, Virginia A. 1995. *Output Measures and More: Planning and Evaluating Public Library Services for Young Adults.* Chicago: American Library Association.

Chapter 6

Setting the Stage for Public Library Young Adult Service

Patrick Jones

One of the first "rules of the thumb" you learn in library school is that "20 percent of the collection answers 80 percent of the questions." What seems obvious but is rarely discussed is that library staff answers 100 percent of those reference questions. That is what makes it a reference question: the human element making the connection between the customer and the collection, print or electronic. Like reference, circulation and readers' advisory transactions are also customer service interactions. Customer service interactions are, in turn, temporary relationships; few patrons are regular users. If there are problems, it seems that many of us spend a great deal of time "blaming" the other person in the relationship—the customer—for those problems or trying to change that person's behavior. Instead, we should focus on what we can change: our side of the relationship and our customer service skills.

Yet, most libraries spend the majority of their time, effort, and professional legitimacy on developing those collections, not developing the people that use them. More ironic is the inverse relationship between budget and effort. The budget of most libraries is about 50 percent on salaries and only 10 percent on those precious collections. But the time in most libraries is not spent developing that staff, as the National Center for Education Statistics found that only 30 percent of libraries offer young adults training (and is that training about serving kids or serving collections?) (National Center for Education Statistics, 1995).

Most public library managers get to be managers because they were good librarians which may (or may not) be the same skill set to manage people to deliver quality customer service. The majority of the space in our professional journals and the majority of the committees in our professional associations deal with books, not people. The coveted committee assignments are book selection committees: in fact, between the Association for Library Services to Children, Young Adult Library Services Association, and Public Library Association there are only a few committees which even touch on services. Not until ALA, YALSA, and the Margaret Edwards Foundation established the Excellence in Customer Services Awards in 1994 was there even a forum to highlight, recognize, and therefore inspire replication of successful services and/or programs designed specifically to reach and meet the needs of the teen customer ("President Franklin Recognizes . . . ," 1994: 370). Even as wonderful as that project is, it defines customer service very broadly; in fact, what is rewarded most are programs, not direct customer service interactions. The majority of these programs dealt with people, not books or even computers. The most successful programs connected YA customers to the library through services.

Even most interview questions for library jobs ask about books and collections, not people. As we try to select the best possible candidates for customer service jobs—people jobs—do we focus on people skills? Resumes and interviews are time-tested, but certainly, the least effective ways to locate the person with the right set of skills for a customer service job. We don't do testing, we don't run scenarios, we normally don't do "behavioral" interviews, and thus we don't do a good job of matching the skills needed for the job with the skills a person has; often we take the person who interviews the best. Sit across a table, name your favorite YA author and reference source, and you have the job. The real questions should be aimed at finding out about the only three things that really matter in serving teenagers: Is the person smart? Is the person creative? Does the person like kids? The great challenge of developing and delivering quality customer services to young adults is, not surprisingly, not about books, technology, or funding, but simply about people. For a myriad of reasons, lots and lots of folks working in public libraries suffer from ephebiphobia.

Ephebiphobia means a fear and loathing of youth (Astroth, 1994: 28–33). Many library staffs contain members, from directors to librarians to the maintenance crew, who suffer from ephebiphobia. This, of course, will negatively impact services toward YAs. It will impact daily "at-the-desk" interaction, yearly planning, and long-term goal setting. It will impact them by classing YAs as a "special user group" and thus making those who want to serve the group develop rationalizations and make a case.

Once you brush aside any user group as "special," then the status quo is to exclude them, putting the onus on those to who want to include them to create support.

When YA services really do get support, not just in words but in deeds and budget priorities, the library landscape is filled with successful customer service models. Read the descriptions of the programs described in Mary Kay Chelton's three *Excellence in Library Services to Young Adults* books (1994; 1997; and 2000) and the common themes of quality YA service become clear:

1. Provides a transition entry and a buffer into adult reading and collections.
2. Responds to the school-related demands of YAs.
3. Involves cooperation between schools and libraries.
4. Encourages reading for personal enrichment and independent learning.
5. Models for other staff delivery of service.
6. Allows for YA participation.
7. Reaches out to at-risk or special groups of YAs.
8. Reacts to social and cultural trends.
9. Advocates for free and equal access for YAs.
10. Contributes to the healthy development of YAs.

Yet, all of these elements describe service as a whole, not just as reference questions asked and answered. Service is *not* just about that particular moment of truth, but instead about the context that creates the ability to make that moment of truth happen—the context that turns a kid into a customer, a teenager into a library user, and a patron into a raving fan.

Librarians are not alone in trying to figure out how to react to the coming onslaught of young adults. Corporate America is asking the exact same question: How do we get all of these teens to buy our product and visit our store? Retailers and librarians alike know that the answer must involve use of the Internet. This is the first totally wired generation. Those coming of age today have probably never done any "research" without the Internet; they have never known the power and the glory of the *Readers Guide*. Teens are online and so are libraries, so we must ensure that they connect.

Clearly, libraries and librarians must change to increase the quantity and the quality of our customer service to youth. New research, new concepts, and new initiatives are creating a landscape that is open to making the needed improvements. But this means giving up what we know, what we are comfortable with, and in many cases what we have a personal stake in. The way things *are* now came about because they were, at one time, an improvement over the way things *were*. That was then, this is now. The ways things *are* won't work if we want new results. If we are to improve, we must first accept change. Step one is developing a personal willingness to change; step two is, in the context of the organization, helping change occur. By looking at these "predictors and outcomes of openness to changes in a reorganizing workplace" (Wanberg and Banas, 2000: 132–142), librarians serving teens can be leaders in creating a new library model to best meet YAs' needs.

Thus, it isn't enough that YA librarians are youth advocates, it is also necessary that we become change agents. By helping our co-workers obtain the necessary tools and by modeling behavior that demonstrates an openness to change, we can become leaders in creating a new type of library for the twenty-first century. And YA librarians are well positioned to perform this role. Libraries are, in many ways, in their adolescence. We're developing the physical parts (computers) but we are having growing pains adjusting to the side effects of change. Like YAs, libraries are works in progress moving from one developmental stage to another. Like teens, we are caught up in discussions concerning independence, excitement, acceptance, and identity. Who are we? What are libraries? What do they do? What should they do? What do we want them to become? The answer is simple: They should connect the world of young adults with the world of information; it is what we do best. That will not, can not, and should not ever change.

REFERENCES

Astroth, Kirk. 1994. "Beyond Ephebiphobia: Problem Adults or Problem Youths?" *Phi Delta Kappan* (January): 28–33.

Chelton, Mary K., ed. 1994. *Excellence in Library Services to Young Adults: The Nation's Top Programs*. Chicago: American Library Association.

———. 1997. *Excellence in Library Services to Young Adults: The Nation's Top Programs*. Second edition. Chicago: American Library Association.

———. 2000. *Excellence in Library Services to Young Adults: The Nation's Top Programs*. Third edition. Chicago: American Library Association, 2000.

National Center for Education Statistics. 1995. *Services and Resources for Children and Young Adults in Public Libraries.* Washington, DC: U.S. Dept. of Education, Office of Educational Research and Improvement, National Center for Education Statistics.

"President Franklin Recognizes Outstanding Youth Programs." 1994. *American Libraries* (April): 370.

Wanberg, Connie, and Joseph T. Banas. 2000. "Predictors and Outcomes of Openness to Changes in a Reorganizing Workplace." *Journal of Applied Psychology* 85, no. 1 (February): 132–142.

Chapter 7

Creating Raving Fans

Patrick Jones

"Just having satisfied customers isn't good enough anymore. You don't own these customers. They're just parked on your doorstep and will be glad to move along when they find something better."
Raving Fans by Ken Blanchard and Sheldon Bowles (1992: 12)

Young adult customer service in the "Internet age" and super bookstore craze presents libraries with a dilemma: competition. Libraries have always faced competition from recreational and other activities. Competition from other activities was seen in one important study as the number one barrier to YA use of libraries (National Center for Education Statistics, 1995). We always knew young adults needed us. Come report time, come homework time, come term paper time, those young adults would flock to our doors. But those days are over.

With computers in homes, schools, and coffee shops, the public library is no longer the only information business in town. For recreational use, the large expanse of the wonderfully lit and designed super bookstore in most communities provides an attractive alternative. Squeezed from both sides, public libraries need to realize that they are not really in the information business or the book business, but the people business. Connecting people and information is what we do. Our job is about developing and maintaining relationships.

And it is a different set of people that we see in our libraries today. The statistics about the digital divide (*Digital Divide Network*, 2000) are not surprising, but certainly should drive library planning, particularly as applied to youth services. Those teens who frequented our libraries five or ten years ago, those teens like *you*, who most likely grew up middle class and white, are disappearing. Teens are staying home with their computers and going to bookstores. Instead, a different type of customer needs our services. These customers might be visiting a library for the first time ever. They don't know about us or what we do. It is our duty to tell them, show them, and impress them, to turn them not just into satisfied customers, but into raving fans. Raving fans will become lifelong users. Raving fans will tell their teachers and parents and their peers about our service. Raving fans, one of whom in 30 or 40 years just might become the mayor or county official deciding our fate.

The raving fans approach, as proposed by Kenneth Blanchard and Sheldon Bowles, presents one model for customer service excellence. It consists of three simple steps:

1. Develop a vision
2. Identify the customer
3. Deliver plus one percent more

This approach seems particularly intriguing for serving young adults because it is flexible, it involves two-way communications, and it involves having a vision of service. YA services are small enough, malleable enough, and manageable enough to react to a vision. The model or vision of young adult services needs to dramatically change with the changing times. Most existing library models cannot meet the demands of today's landscape of technology, information overload, and increased competition.

DEVELOPING A VISION

So what is a vision of young adult services? What does it look like? Walk in the door of your library and find the young adult area. Is there one? Or does the whole building purport to support young adults? Does the YA area look like a traditional library or something else? Where are the computers? Where are the magazines? Where is the service desk? Is there a service desk or is staff circulating around? If you build it, will they come? Thus, the first rule of raving fans: decide what you want, develop a vision.

The YALSA Vision

There are already visions out there: The YALSA vision, the Satisfaction vision, the Connections vision, the Cool Libraries vision, and the Planning for Results vision. In 1994, the Young Adult Library Services Association adopted the following vision:

> *In every library in the nation, quality library services to young adults are provided by a staff that understands and respects the unique informational, educational, and recreational needs of teenagers. Equal access to information, services, and materials is recognized as a right not a privilege. Young adults are actively involved in the library decision-making process. The library staff collaborates and cooperates with other youth-serving agencies to provide a holistic communitywide network of activities services that supports healthy youth development (YALSA Vision Statement, 2000).*

Let's pick that vision apart to understand the roots of what this new service will look like. The first statement "in every library" is just that—a vision. Research tells us that fewer than 15 percent of public libraries have a young adult librarian (National Center for Education Statistics, 1995: 16), even though we know that just about every public library serves teenagers. No public library boldly pastes a sticker on the front of their annual report that says "except for teenagers," even though in practice teens are essentially excluded from the daily business of librarics. They are excluded through poor service, through outdated materials, through collection development concepts developed and best suited for children, and through an attitude that suggests toleration rather than true consideration of their unique needs and wants. They are excluded by the lack of any real commitment to serve them.

The second word to define is "quality," which is a book in itself (see *Zen and The Art of Motorcycle Maintenance* by Robert Pirsig [1974]). We normally define quality in terms of quantity, and there is some truth in that approach. If circulation goes up, if the number of tours increases, and program attendance doubles, we feel those services must be representative of "quality" programs and services since they are well used. The problem is most libraries can't, don't, and even won't define quality because they feel they can't measure it. Or as Kevin Elliot writes in *Journal of Customer Service in Marketing and Management*, "if an organization cannot effectively measure quality performance, it will not be able to manage it" (1995: 35). A simple definition of quality relates back to a simple definition of purpose. People "buy" two things when they buy a service: solutions to problems and good feelings. The true mark of quality is how well we solve those problems and how many good feelings we elicit. Thus, defining quality means developing methods to capture it.

The Satisfaction Vision

Peter Hernon and Ellen Altman's vision of quality is radically different since it focuses on customer expectation, not library outputs or ideals. Their *Assessing Service Quality: Satisfying the Expectations of Library Customers* boldly states in the preface that

> The library community needs to shift its focus from measuring and reporting volume of business, such as for circulation, to more meaningful indicators of customer loyalty, expectations, preferences, and satisfaction. The new indicators should report information about present and potential customers, their needs, expectations, and preferences, as well as the problems they encounter and how staff handles those problems. Such information is useful for promoting customer loyalty, enhancing the service reputation of libraries, and for planning and decision making. Customers are more than a source for data collection, they are the reason for libraries' existence. It is important (if not essential) to listen to, and learn from, customers and to use the insights gained to improve services (Hernon and Altman, 1998: iv).

The book then goes on to explore, in great detail, how to make this shift of emphasis from collection to customer occur by looking at mission statements, customer surveys, complaint management, focus groups, looking at the differences between satisfaction and service quality, and finally embracing change. Using research, over one hundred charts and figures, and providing a clear and consistent message, Hernon and Altman make a strong case for a new vision of all library services that argues "unless customers and the collection come together in a way both interesting and meaningful to the customer, the library is nothing more than an expensive warehouse" (1998: 6).

The Connections Vision

The challenge of this vision, however, is to get our library boards or city councils to accept it, since they have been weaned on how many and how much for years. Thus, how do we balance (and measure) the expectations and satisfaction of customers with the expectations and satisfaction of our funders? If we can't go directly to customer satisfaction (how many libraries report the statistics on customer satisfaction along with circulation numbers to funding agencies?), then let's look at what we can do as an interim step.

Customer service, as stated, is about connections. Yes, also as stated, those connections are being made on a moving train. Continuing to report circulation as our "prime number" is a losing battle as most public libraries report decline in circulation in the face of the Internet ("Public Library Circulation Dips . . . ," 1999: 69). Look at your own library. Has not circulation dropped now that a teen can come in and print out a page about the Alamo from the Internet rather than checking out a book? There is a growing field concerned with measuring electronic use (Hiott, 1999: 44-47) that seeks to capture that number; but again, circulation represents only a part of what we do. The biggest factor in what we measure, it seems, is what we do well. But the fact is that we do lots of things well, other than circulate materials. In particular, the role of a branch library in an inner city does lots of important things that add value to the community and to the lives of teens which have nothing to do with circulating books. These branches may offer tutoring, homework assistance, or simply Internet access. They may be tied into the social services network for job training or they may collaborate with local agencies that offer human services—or they may simply offer a safe haven.

Let's look instead at libraries reporting for youth services, not just YA but all youth services—a connections number. This number would consist of the total number of connections made through:

- Program attendance
- Participation in an after-school program
- Reference
- Circulation
- Hits to library-created youth Web pages
- Hits to subscription databases (Electric Library©, etc.)
- Overall computer use (Internet, word processing, educational games, etc.)
- In-house use of materials
- Library card registration
- Outreach attendance

What we measure are connections between people, customer service interactions—or call them relationships. We wish to capture all the different ways the library staff connects kids to information. It counts regardless if the connection occurs in the public library, in a school, in a day care, in an outreach van visiting a park, or through the Internet. Let's look at a hypothetical month (the numbers are made up, pure speculation; what matters is the process) for YA services as it is probably reported now in most public libraries:

MEASURE	COUNT
Circulation	2,000
Reference	3,500

Those that value outreach and programming might also add:

MEASURE	COUNT
Program	125
Outreach	500

A system with more resources to do an after-school program might choose to report participation. Other factors, which often get counted, are in-house use and library card registration.

MEASURE	COUNT
After school	150
In-house	700
Library cards	200

All of these reflect double counting as all library statistics have always done. We don't not count a book that circulates because we already counted the interaction which led to the book circulating; we don't not count the circulation of people who attend programs, and we don't discount the in-house use of folks who ask reference questions. We are measuring *what* people do in our building, not just where or who they do it with.

Finally, libraries should also investigate electronic use:

Databases	1,200
Web hits	900
Computer use	1,750

Now that we have this data, what do we do with it? Why don't we total it and begin reporting a "connections number"? This number reflects the most basic thing we do in libraries in the twenty-first century: connecting people to information. This data values technology, it values outreach, and it still values circulating books. Our efforts should be to increase *this* number, not just circulation. The number we start using, benchmarking, and caring about isn't just circulation, but all the ways we connect with youth.

MEASURE	COUNT
Circulation	2,000
Reference	3,500
Program	125
Outreach	500
After school	150
In-house	700
Library cards	200
Databases	1,200
Web hits	900
Computer use	1,750
TOTAL	11,025

This does three things:

1. It moves away from focusing on circulation, an area that is sure to decline.
2. It shows our funders *all* that we do, while at the same time takes in the holistic ways in which teenagers use libraries. Unlike many adults and children who may settle into routine patterns of library use, teenagers could in a given week or month get connected in every way. We then start looking at applying ratios: number of connections per kid and then *that* becomes the one number we aim to increase. It takes the very broad number and shows direct impact on a customer.
3. This vision allows branches/units with different strengths to be recognized for those strengths. Traditionally, for example, a small older branch in an inner city neighborhood will certainly not report the same circulation as a big new suburban branch, so naturally that branch is "looked down on" by administrators who look only at circulation numbers and only value outreach as a means to increasing circulation. But that branch could be making just as many connections (again, per capita) as the bigger branch if they are doing more outreach, if they have an active after-school program, and/or if they work more with the kids using computers. Let's compare two such imaginary branches.

LARGE SUBURBAN		SMALL INNER CITY	
MEASURE	**COUNT**	**MEASURE**	**COUNT**
Circulation	5,000	Circulation	1,000
Reference	2,000	Reference	1,500
Program	75	Program	500
Outreach	0	Outreach	3,000
After school	0	After school	500
In-house	700	In-house	500
Library cards	100	Library cards	150
Databases	1,500	Databases	1,000
Web hits	775	Web hits	1,000
Computer use	1,000	Computer use	2,000
TOTAL	**11,150**	**TOTAL**	**11,150**

Thus, when we compare the two service units on all measures of connections, they could both make a very similar impact. If we go one step further, and divide the total connections number by the budget, square footage of the YA section, YA staff hours, volumes, and open hours, we might find the small inner city library is actually getting "more bang for the buck" or "more connections for the cash" than the large suburban library.

4. Finally, this vision is about how we report information. We take that connecting number, total it, and then figure percentages for each element. Thus, our monthly reports now all feature a chart like this:

Chart 7.1: Connection Count

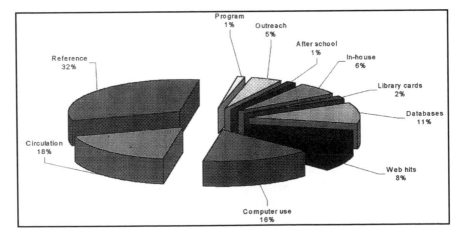

We tell our funders that we are in the customer business, the connections business, and this is how we do it.

Just as important, we put these things on a "straight line" of equal value. Is there and should there be more "value" placed on connecting with a kid by teaching how to use the Internet during a session at school as opposed to that same kid coming into the library checking out a book? They represent the same amount of effort and cost, a measure of value; it is just a matter of who is making that effort and absorbing the cost. Thus, another vision of YA customer service is one that captures, measures, and celebrates our connections.

The Cool Libraries Vision

Another vision of quality was recently offered from the findings of the Reader's Digest DeWitt Wallace Partners in Youth Development project. Based on surveys, interviews, and focus groups with teens from ten urban libraries, a vision of "cool libraries" emerged. Cool libraries would:

- Be bright, cheerful, and filled with varied activities
- Have music rooms and videos rooms
- Offer longer weekend and evening hours
- Rethink fines and other regulations
- Give teens a place of their own (Meyer, 1999: 35)

The vision that teens have of cool public libraries would focus on several key areas of technology, space, collections, and youth involvement. In technology, the vision would have more computers, more printers, better and newer software, unlimited Internet access on all computers, and the right tools for a true multimedia experience (shockwave software, headphones, etc.). For space, the vision includes better and more comfortable furniture, a more appealing look, much better lighting, lots of multi-use space for both quiet and group study, vending machines, and an area that is created and maintained for/by young adults. The vision of the collection is one filled with magazines, media of all forms, and lots of new books, as well as multiple copies of titles needed for assignments. Better arrangement of materials coupled with better-looking materials complete the materials vision. All these visions are wonderful, yet the teen surveys noted the frustration of library rules limiting not just the vision but access. Their vision includes making library hours that are more attractive to students, policies on fines that allow for flexibility, and a less restrictive overall atmosphere. Their responses suggested that libraries seem focused only on negatives ("no this" and "don't do that") rather than on positives. Finally, the vision involves allowing teens to help implement this dream library through internships, community service learning, volunteering, or through youth councils. Teens who care about libraries are willing to work to make them better and spread the word. In essence, the vision of a "cool library" provides the second key step in the raving fans process: finding out what the customer wants.

The Planning for Results Vision

Another model for envisioning YA service in public libraries is provided by *Planning for Results: A Public Library Transformation Process*. An expansion and revision of the *Role Setting for Public Library* approach, this new process examines not roles but service responses. The definition of a service response is "what a library does, or offers to the public, in an effort to meet a well-defined community need" (*Planning for Results*, 1998: 54). The best use of service responses is in the context of the overall planning process. These service responses are, in essence, the vision of what a public library can be in the community. Let's take each service response and look for the "YA angle" to see how teen customers could benefit from each:

Basic Literacy—A library that offers basic literacy service addresses the need to read and to perform other essential daily tasks.

> A library with basic literacy as a primary service response is probably in an area of high poverty and/or a community containing recent non-English speaking immigrants. A YA response would be to have materials, tutors, and instructional software available to help these teens gain literacy skills. After-school, weekend, and outreach programs promoting literacy coupled with partnerships in the community with agencies having similar missions would characterize this service response. They might focus on high school dropouts by providing GED classes and complement those efforts with a collection containing basic skill books/workbooks as well as high-interest/low-vocabulary materials. This role positions the library as a leader in the community in helping teenagers learn the most basic of skills. That is the programmatic response. The relationship response is to realize that printed material shouldn't be the only option we provide or offer during a reference interview. The unfortunate double-whammy is that the proliferation of the Internet and subscription databases hit illiterate and semi-literate teens doubly hard: they lack technology skills and even if they had them, they couldn't read the words on the screen.

Business and Career Information—A library that offers business and career information services addresses a need for information related to business, careers, work, personal finances, and obtaining employment.

> The career information center is a key YA role, particularly in areas with high unemployment among teens. A library choosing this role should work closely with the high schools, vo-tech schools, adult education (in particular, ESL and GED sections), and community workforce agencies to develop and plan this service. Further, as stated earlier, employing students to work in our libraries in a wide variety of tasks, not just shelving books or taping magazines, could play a dominant part in a library undertaking this role.

Commons Environment—A library that provides a commons environment helps address the need of people to meet and interact with others in their community and to participate in public discourse about community issues.

> A library assuming this role can easily provide a teen focus. By becoming involved in community issues such as youth violence, development assets, and the like, the library can be seen as a central place to meet to discuss, but also to play a role in solving such issues. By providing a neutral ground, public libraries can bring together representatives from different schools and youth-serving agencies to discuss these issues. The commons concept also works well for libraries that develop after-school programs, youth advisory groups, and/or conducts teen focus groups. In all instances, the library is playing a central role in pulling teens from different parts of the community together for a common purpose. Finally, the commons many teens seek is to meet and interact with other teens online. Chat-only, Internet-only equipment possibly coupled with a coffee bar would be the very definition of a teen commons.

Community Referral—A library that offers community referral addresses the need for information related to services provided by community agencies and organizations.

> Public libraries could either take a lead role in setting up "Teen Yellow Pages" in print or, better yet, on the Web. Working with the United Way or similar agencies that exist in most communities, the library can help gather, organize, and disseminate information about the community to teens. Also, getting on the mailing list for organi-

zations to send notices of events, lectures, and the like, as well as to receive give-away informational pamphlets on health, sexuality, etc., can be vital for serving teens with the best, most current information available on these vital topics.

Consumer Information—A library that provides consumer information addresses the need for information to make informed consumer decisions and helps residents become more self-sufficient.

The business research tells us that teens are heavily involved in making big-ticket decisions, in particular when it comes to technology. Helping teens help their parents choose computers, online service providers, etc., as well as teaching them how to find consumer information online, would be essential services to provide here.

Cultural Awareness—A library that provides cultural awareness services helps satisfy the desire of community residents to gain an understanding of their own cultural heritage and the cultural heritage of others.

Libraries that offer after-school programming for teens are perfectly positioned to create programs to celebrate diversity during the various heritage months (Hispanic Heritage month during September/October, Black Heritage month in February, and Asian Heritage month in May). In addition, cultural festivals in the community provide a wonderful outreach opportunity to get the library "out front" and visible in their community. In addition to libraries' print collections, diversity can be celebrated through the selection of music, videos, and in creating Web pages.

Current Topics and Titles—A library that provides current topics and titles helps to fulfill community residents' appetite for information and popular culture, social trends, and their desire for satisfying recreational experiences.

A library choosing this role is locked into YA services since, with the exception of *New York Times* best sellers list (that is before *Harry Potter*, the Rock, and Mankind), almost all popular culture is teen driven. Stephen King, John Grisham, and Mary Higgins Clark sell lots of books to teens, particularly in paperback. In addition to books, current titles and topics should extend to both non-print and magazines. Libraries that can react best to trends will score big with teens.

If we can organize ourselves so that we can quickly obtain, process, and circulate the latest pop culture craze, we can do a huge service to teens. If we can't, we do a disservice to our customers and, if it takes six months to acquire and process the Ricky Martin biographies, the *Scream* movie tie-ins, or the *High Fidelity* movie soundtrack, we have likely wasted our limited resources because the pop market will have changed. To a greater degree than adults or children, teens want what is hot now and are not willing to wait. And they shouldn't need to. By using a magazine like *Entertainment Weekly* as a selection tool, by subscribing to various "alert" services available from online booksellers like Amazon, and by using jobber catalogs rather than only traditional library review sources, we can meet this need. If your selection policy requires two or three positive reviews and one of them will be *Booklist* (which rarely touches half of true YA pop culture since most of this material is *not* produced by traditional library publishers), we will always be "so five minutes ago."

Formal Learning Support—A library that offers formal learning support helps students who are enrolled in a formal program of education or who are pursuing their education through a program of home schooling to obtain educational goals.

This is the big one. If we don't do well in supporting formal learning, we are sunk. And it is not that hard. First, let's give up on pie-in-the-sky ideas like getting assignments from teachers ahead of time and of having enough copies of the books everyone needs. And while we're at it, let's chuck our condescending mock amazement at students' lack of planning. We know we can't make real changes in the behavior of students or teachers, so now what? Let's start putting together assignment notebooks. Let's gather information not from teachers, but from students as we encounter them over the reference desk about assignments: What are the objectives? What are the requirements? Let's use these notebooks to answer these mass assignment questions more efficiently, to develop assignment-specific Web pages, to order materials for when the assignments come again next year, and finally to be pro-active in this role. Let's stop whining and do the work that needs to be done to meet and support the needs of these teens whose "job" is called school.

General Information—A library that offers general information helps meet the need for information and answers to questions on a broad array of topics related to work, school, and personal life.

This role, with its reference to topics related to school certainly makes it a YA role. But there is the nice reminder here about information for personal life, or lifework as opposed to homework. Yet, another reason to have a YA area is to stock titles like:

- Abner, Allison. *Finding Our Way: The Teen Girls Survival Guide.* 1996. Harperperennial Library.
- Basso, Michael. *The Underground Guide to Teenage Sexuality.* 1997. Fairview Press.
- Benson, Peter. *What Teens Need to Succeed.* 1998. Free Spirit Publishing.
- Canfield, D. *Chicken Soup for the Teenage Soul.* 1997. Health Communications.
- Chandler, Kurt. *Passengers of Pride: Lesbian and Gay Youth Come of Age.* 1997. Alyson.
- Hirsch, Karen. *Mind Riot: Coming of Age in Comix.* 1997. Aladdin.
- Pratt, Jane. *Beyond Beauty: Girls Speak Out on Looks, Style, and Stereotypes.* 1997. Clarkson Potter.
- Roberts, Tara. *Am I the Last Virgin? Ten African American Reflections on Sex and Love.* 1997. Aladdin.
- Rubin, Nancy. *Ask Me If I Care? Voices from an American High School.* 1994. Ten Speed Press.
- Salinger, Adrienne. *My Room: Teenagers in Their Bedrooms.* 1995. Chronicle Books.
- Schiller, Lori. *The Quiet Room: A Journey Out of the Torment of Madness.* 1996. Warner.

Government Information—A library that offers government information service helps satisfy the need for information about elected officials and governmental agencies that enables people to participate in the democratic process.

On the face of it, there is not that much here which speaks to YA needs, with the exception of working with high school civics and government classes to ensure that the information collected in this area becomes a real learning tool to allow young people to participate in the democratic process. Beneath the surface, however, one can find a wealth of information relevant to teens and their needs from a plethora of governmental agencies. Resources formerly only available in print through fairly Byzantine, time-consuming, paid-in-advance channels are now often available online, instantly at no cost.

For both personal and school-related topics, government information can be a gold mine for inquisitive teens.

Information Literacy—A library that provides information literacy services helps address the need for skills related to finding, evaluating, and using information efficiently.

> This needs to become a major role for the American public library if it is to survive. Information literacy gets at the core of what we do, which is connecting people and information. One way we do that is by teaching the necessary skills to make that connection happen. Necessary skills are no longer just how to "find" information, but how to evaluate it and, to a lesser extent, what to do with it. There is a *huge* amount of literature on this role, but most of it relates to the school library. Your first task is to go over to the school library and learn what is being taught. Is information literacy in the curriculum? If not, then what can you do to help make it happen? How is information literacy being taught? Is the school librarian using the Big Six or another model? If so, learn it and use it. Technology affords so many more avenues for cooperation and resource sharing/development. Do this: construct a "how to use the XYZ public library Web page" for the key grades. Include basic stuff on catalog, magazines, etc., and ask the school librarian to link to the Web page; and then use it during instruction sessions.

Lifelong Learning—A library that provides lifelong learning services helps address the desire for self-directed personal growth and development opportunities.

> This, too, is a vital YA role. Notice that lifelong learning doesn't mean "adult," which is great because teens are using public library collections for information on personal interests. Learning how to build Web pages, how to paint or draw, how to write poetry, or how to do almost anything could be included under this umbrella statement. But I would argue that fiction, in particular genre fiction, falls under the scope of this role. Teens read fiction for recreation, but also for emotional and developmental reasons. The kids who read fantasy usually become lifelong readers of that genre, similar with series romances. The key to genre fiction is that readers respond to it. Their response is what drives them to read it, to read another book and then another, and to become lifelong readers. By definition then,

reading genre fiction is all about self-directed personal growth and development opportunities. If you are, or know people who are, of the opinion that genre fiction stunts growth, I would refer you to *What's So Scary About R.L. Stine* (Jones, 1998) where I examined years of reading research finding that this is one of those myths that flies directly into the teeth of the facts.

Local History and Genealogy—A library that offers local history and genealogy services addresses the desire of community residents to know and better understand personal or community heritage.

This area may not be a prime focus of collection development efforts for YAs, but if the adult patrons of your community demand and use such materials you might find that teens in your school avail themselves of it at times to complete school assignments. Cultural history, personal history, and community history are often topics that are part of social studies classes at the junior high and high school level.

These five visions are starters. Your vision will be different based upon community needs, your own philosophy of service, YA input, and the overall library's mission. But you need a vision. Think about what you want YA services to look like, sound like, and feel like. Regardless of what your vision entails, it must speak to those moments of truth when the library staff and teens interact. While in some ways the vision is large and institutional, it comes down to the personal; to the one-on-one interaction. All the planning of floor space, all the collection development, and all the training provide the context for the moment of truth.

IDENTIFYING THE CUSTOMER

There are two parts to this process. The first is to identify who the customer is; the second is to identify what they want. We have a good amount of information on who the YA customer is in public libraries, although it is getting a little long in the tooth, from the last national survey conducted by the U.S. Department of Education in 1995 (National Center for Education Statistics, 1995), which surveyed over 800 public libraries of all sizes and from every geographic area.

Each library should conduct its own survey to establish benchmarks that describe where they are and to provide guidance on where they should be going. While not addressing library services as a whole, but rather just gathering information for collection development decisions, I conducted a survey during Teen Read Week of over 3,000 students in Houston. The survey was conducted in three formats. It was available online, to which over 500 self-reporting YAs responded. It was also available in a paper format and was distributed in every branch library as well as given out/collected by several teachers. Over 1,500 of the paper surveys were returned. Finally, over 1,000 students were administered the survey in person during the booktalking visits. While this technique is not perfect, since it might involve too much groupthink, it does show how easy and how available the opportunities are to collect this type of data. The gender breakdown ended up almost 50/50. While I didn't report demographic breakdown overall, I know that most of the classes I visited during Teen Read Week were at schools which reflected the demographics of Houston: most of them were made up largely of Hispanic students, except for a few schools which were primarily African American. Few of these public schools had Anglo students, although the one private school was almost entirely white.

The questions asked were:

- How old are you?
- What is your favorite reading material?
- What is your favorite type of book?
- What is your favorite type of fiction?
- What is your favorite type of nonfiction?
- How do you find out about new books?

The methodology to gather these findings was way too "loose" to call it research, but I was not interested in gathering information to publish in a refereed journal, but rather information to help the selectors choose from the offerings of various publishers. This data is a gold mine and to run various analyses by looking at responses by age or gender would have been great information to have collected, but just icing. The cake is here: the teens surveyed like magazines, horror fiction, true crime and pop culture, and choose books by browsing. We probably already "knew" that, but surveys like this allow us to really "know" it.

Acting on the assumption (which from Altman and Hernon we know is probably incorrect, not to mention wrongheaded) that one method of measuring YA customer satisfaction is through use, and that the best measure of use we have is circulation, then how do we increase that number, thus increase customer satisfaction? There are only two ways to increase circulation in a library:

1. Get the people coming in to check out more
2. Get more people to come in, then see #1

The question I didn't ask during these surveys was how many YAs get materials to read from the public library. Given what I know about those communities and about the circulation of materials at branches in many of those communities, I would say those surveyed were mainly not library users. I will guess that one reason that magazines rate so high was not for all the usual reasons that kids like magazines, but mainly because it was the only reading materials these kids had easy access to since you can buy magazines at every convenience store (notice that most store magazine offerings cater to young adults. One store I just visited had nothing but wrestling, music, and teen magazines). And no, these kids were not getting books from their sadly, rather dismally stocked and funded school libraries or buying them from Amazon—and most do not have a bookstore anywhere near by. So, we combine the question of vision with that of audience in deciding where to dedicate our resources: improving the collections for the YAs currently using our libraries or improving the collections to attract those not using the library? The rub, of course, is we can't afford to do both.

Thus, it also comes down to a question of where to place our priorities, with users or non-users, and to identity their needs and wants.

YA Needs

- Hang out
- Socialize
- Bathroom
- Study
- Find info homework
- Find info lifework
- Get served
- Find a book or magazine
- Communicate with others
- Place to stay warm/cool and safe

YA Wants

- Fiction for fun
- Nonfiction for interests
- Music to listen
- Videos to watch
- Magazines/comics books to read

- Internet access
- Friendly environment
- Programs of interest
- Chances to participate
- Positive experience

One more list. Let's look at what YAs, in particular young adolescents, want and need from a developmental perspective. With the possible exception of "physical activity," all those on the following list are YA wants and needs that libraries can address. Understanding these needs are the reasons that teens are *who* they are and *why* they are, and thus impacts our moments of truth with them. For example, it is a time of self-definition. If every YA is a star in their own movie, as has been suggested, then think about the "library set." On the most basic level, a teen that must approach a reference desk to pose a reference question is almost assuming the position of a supplicant (I need help, ergo I am helpless; you can help me, ergo you have a power and are more powerful than I.) Is that something a teen wants to do? Of course not, thus many a YA never get to a moment of truth encounter because they won't ask for help. Proactive reference, being out on the floor, looking for kids who look stuck or lost, asking "Are you finding what you need?" rather than "Do you need help?" (ergo, you are helpless), and having lots and lots of signage and point-of-use instruction combat the YA tendency not to ask for help. So, the list of what YAs want and need in their lives contains·

- Physical activity
- Competence and achievement

Action Plan #7: Assess the Needs

Assess the needs of teens in your community. Do the lists above completely answer your question? Probably not completely given the diversity of various communities. So think about it. What are the basic needs and wants young adults in your community have for the public library that are not listed above? Brainstorm, call a meeting, convene a focus group, or just hang out at the mall and ask some teens what they are doing there today. Show them your list and ask for their input. Share the results with your staff and plan accordingly to provide for the needs and wants of the teens in your community.

- Self-definition
- Creative expression
- Positive social interaction with peers and adults
- Structure and clear limits
- Meaningful participation (Vaillancourt, 1999: 112)

When planning programs, when thinking about training, and even when putting together collections, this "big seven" list represents the most basic level of identifying our customer, and thus preparing our responses. When we look at program development, these seven needs manifest themselves in another set of needs that are considered essential requirements for healthy adolescents:

- Find a place of value in a constructive group
- Learn how to form close, durable human relationships
- Feel a sense of worth as a person
- Achieve a reliable basis for making informed choices
- Know how to use the support systems available to them
- Express constructive curiosity and exploratory behavior
- Find ways of being useful to others
- Believe in a promising future with real opportunity
- Master social skills, including the ability to manage conflict peacefully
- Cultivate the inquiring and problem-solving habits for lifelong learning
- Acquire the technical and analytical capabilities to participate in a world-class economy
- Become an ethical person
- Learn the requirements of responsible citizenship
- Respect diversity in our pluralistic society (Carnegie Council on Adolescent Development, 1992)

Our responses to each of these will, more than likely, involve programs and collections. The collection may not be book or print based, which is good because one of the wants/needs of many adolescents is simply to be literate.

From developing a vision and then identifying the customers wants and needs, we've set the stage to start delivering service.

Action Plan #8: The Good, the Bad, and the Ugly.

Reflect on customer service interactions you have had that stand out in your mind. Waitresses and waiters, salespeople, whomever. Can you recall a "good" transaction? What was it and *what* made it good? How about a bad one? Finally, how about an ugly one? *Ugly* meaning it led you to take action of some sort, such as writing a letter of complaint or resolving not to patronize that business ever again. Keep those stories in mind as you read through this section, and especially keep them in mind as you find yourself delivering services from the "other side" of the customer service counter.

DELIVERING PLUS ONE PERCENT MORE

Delivering starts with making a serious commitment to adopting a customer service philosophy, plan, and practice. It is not just what we do on the desk, but what we do before getting to the desk: the total context of a customer service plan. True, a YA customer service plan *should* be part of an overall library plan, but don't wait. Implement it today to keep these customers for life. But what does "one percent more" mean? "One percent more" doesn't mean going the extra mile, but just the extra step. It means taking the time, which might be all of ten seconds, to ensure that each YA customer receives superior service. It is setting up homework centers, doing after-school programs, building YA Web pages, handing out business cards, and closing the question with a smile. It is simply the necessary things to make that moment of truth turn out the best for the YA customer and for the library.

Key steps for creating a service orientation culture for young adults begins with hiring good people. Consider looking for people who have customer service experience and obviously *like* kids. Look for flexibility, creativity, intelligence, enthusiasm, and a sense of humor. A mistake made too frequently in interviews is that we listen only to *what* people say, not *how* they say it. A person who tells you they are excited about working with kids in a dull monotone, probably isn't. A person who talks about the importance of a sense of humor, but has none, again, might not be a good fit.

So, how do you capture these things? First, decide what skills you are looking for and then ask questions that will help you determine if the candidate has those skills to offer. Make sure you are doing a structured interview so everyone is asked the same question. While asking questions like "Name your favorite authors" are pretty standard, they don't really fit into what you are looking for, unless you ask candidates why they like those authors, why they think kids would also like them, and how they could connect kids with those authors. An interview for a customer service position needs to be a behavioral interview asking the candidate to describe an incident where they exhibited the skills you are looking for in the job. This will get you specific examples as opposed to textbook answers. It will show you *how* a person solves problems. You can also ask them to solve problems by posing scenarios. Here are some sample interview questions for hiring someone who can create raving YA fans. (By this point in the book, you should have a good idea of what the "right" answer is to each of these):

- Pretend I am a young adult who is a first time user of this library and who needs a book to use for a book report due tomorrow. What questions would you ask me and *why*?
- Tell me your *best* customer service interaction with a young adult. Now, tell me your worst.
- Describe an experience where you worked with an angry or dissatisfied customer and how you resolved the situation.
- If you wanted to increase use of the young adult collection by 20 percent in one year's time, what changes would you make today?
- Describe an experience where you worked in an organization undergoing a great deal of change. What role did you play in the change process and how did you "cope" with the changes?
- A YA patron asks you, "Where can I buy a term paper?" What would be your response?
- What are the three most important qualities in working with young adults? Now, describe from your experiences how you have demonstrated each.
- Teens today are very "techno savvy." Describe an experience you have had in helping a young adult use information technology.
- A YA customer comes in five minutes before the library is closing and needs five books, three magazine articles, and an Internet citation on a topic. What is your response?
- How will you ensure that every YA who walks through the door receives quality customer service?
- When you were a young adult, were you a library user? If so, why? If not, why not?
- What question should we have asked you?
- If you could describe yourself in one word, what would it be?

Second, set standards for performance—these are called performance reviews. I could write another book on the lousy job most libraries do on performance reviews; so again, you might be caught in a bad system. Here are a couple of ideas: encourage "360 reviews" involving everyone above and below the person being reviewed in the process. If people know they are "performing" before their peers, it might just improve performance. Talk to patrons about performance. Ask the "regular" kids who on the reference staff treats them best. Finally, if you've followed the advice to set up a simple comment card program, set a standard that requires each librarian to receive at least five positive comment cards in a year's period from teenagers. This will encourage the librairian to hand out the cards (goal one achieved!) and to provide better customer service (goal two!).

Third, educate the customer. Face it, most teens have no idea of the scope of what we can do. We need to educate them to the opportunities. Start by coming up with a user education plan directed at one user group; maybe one grade, one school, or maybe with a community agency or recent immigrant teens. Set learning objectives and do evaluations to ensure that your message is getting through. Education can be active (tours, presentations) or passive (image map of Web pages or even just a map of the library). Act on the assumption that most users don't understand *what* we do or *how* we do it.

Fourth, conduct internal assessments. In *Putting Service Into Library Staff Training*, Joanna Bessler suggests the following "internal audit" to help focus everyone on recognizing good service:

- My supervisor praises me when I make a special effort to help a patron solve a problem
- I feel my supervisor wants me to rush my work; quantity seems more important than quality
- When I bend a policy to help a patron, I am praised if my supervisor likes my decision
- Merit raises are directly tied to excellence
- People who might be described as "people champions" are promoted
- I learn about the service contributions of other staff at library meetings
- I learn about the service contributions of other staff through written communication
- My annual performance review includes comments on my service contributions (Bessler, 1994: 45)

Lastly, make service results visible. Be proud of achievements. Post circulation and reference statistics for the public to see. Post comment cards with the names blacked out. Let people know you are improving.

Action Plan #9:The Menu

Look over the above five steps for creating a good customer service environment for teens. List ways you can begin implementing them this week, over the next three months, and before the end of the next year.

REFERENCES

Bessler, Joanne. 1994. *Putting Service into Library Staff Training : A Patron-Centered Guide.* Chicago: American Library Association.

Blanchard, Ken, and Sheldon Bowles. 1992. *Raving Fans: A Revolutionary Approach to Customer Service.* New York: William Morrow & Co.

Carnegie Council on Adolescent Development. 1992. *A Matter of Time: Risk and Opportunities in the Nonschool Hours.* New York: Carnegie Corporation.

Digital Divide Network. 2000. [Online]. Available *www.digitaldividenetwork.org/* [August 18].

Elliot, Kevin. 1995. "A Comparison of Alternative Measures of Service Quality." *Journal of Customer Service in Marketing and Management* 1, no. 1: 35.

Hernon, Peter, and Ellen Altman. (1998). *Assessing Service Quality: Satisfying the Expectations of Library Customers.* Chicago: American Library Association.

Hiott, Judith. 1999. "Making Online Use Count." *Library Journal* (October 1): 44-47.

Jones, Patrick. 1998. *What's So Scary About R.L. Stine?* Lanham, MD: Scarecrow Press.

Meyer, Elaine. 1999. "Cool Libraries." *American Libraries* (November): 35.

National Center for Education Statistics. 1995. *Services and Resources for Children and Young Adults in Public Libraries.* Washington, DC: U.S. Dept. of Education, Office of Educational Research and Improvement, National Center for Education Statistics.

Pirsig, Robert. 1974. *Zen and The Art of Motorcycle Maintenance: An Inquiry into Values.* New York: William Morrow.

Planning For Results: A Public Library Transformation Process. 1998. Chicago: American Library Association.

"Public Library Circulation Dips As Spending Continues to Climb." 1999. *American Libraries* (September): 69.

Vaillancourt, Renee J. 1999. *Bare Bones Young Adult Services: Tips for Public Library Generalists.* Second edition. Chicago: American Library Association.

YALSA Vision Statement. 2000. [Online]. Available *www.ala.org/yalsa/about/vision.html* [August 18].

Chapter 8

Lessons from the Mall

Patrick Jones

"It's the first generation that grew up with technology and they're totally comfortable with it" ("Tracking Teens," 1999: 6+).

Business literature is rich with articles about customer service to teens. Well aware of the spending power of teens, coupled with the coming population explosion, trade journals and business news magazines have been running a constant stream of articles on all facets of reaching the teen market. While certainly not every aspect of the business model for teen customer service can or will apply to a public library setting, there are lessons to be learned from "the mall" that may just hold the key to success to connecting young adults and libraries. The two big "issues" that appear in the business literature are the same two which are of interest to librarians: how to attract the growing teen market to our "store" and how to reach them online. Let's look at quotes from various business publications about these two areas, and then consider three things to do to improve customer service to teens.

TEENS AND THE INTERNET

"The main thing teens look for on the Internet is speed: speed of the computer, speed of the connection, and speed in finding information. When teens go online to look for something very specific, if a site takes too long to download, they're gone" (Cogner, 1999: 2a+).

1. As we do collection development for our Web pages, we need to keep the consideration of speed close at hand. Maybe it means not pointing to the "Front page," which can be eye-catching but graphic and plug-in heavy, but rather to the first "real" page of a site. We need to make sure that as we review pages, we review them on the same computers the customers will use, not our own. We need to see how these pages will look when they come up for the customers.

2. Our Web pages should always list hot links for the most popular topics prominently, such as at the top of the page. The big mistake most YA Web pages make is trying to include "everything." It is better instead to include the top five or ten links that point kids to the information site they need and then build separate pages with more links for those who are not satisfied or need more than those first few links provide. Similarly, don't drown the page in graphic files. Yes, the page needs to have graphics to appeal to YA users, but keep the file sizes small. The more graphics and the larger they are, the slower it takes to download. The slower to download, the faster your YA user will click "stop" and move on to another page.

3. Encourage more downloading and less printing to speed up time spent on terminals. Floppy disks are cheap, repairing over-worked printers and buying reams of paper and caseloads of ink cartridges are not. In instruction, focus on timesaving tricks, including e-mailing citations and full-text articles, when licensing allows, from databases to home e-mail accounts. Show kids how to download a Web page or graphics file. Show them how they can convert a Web page into a Word document. Show them how to cut and paste from a Web page into Word. Show them how to bookmark sites and save the bookmark file to disk. By setting up our Internet areas as printing areas, not only do we slow everyone down (and frustrate folks who *hate* the amount of "wasteful" printing), we fail to teach kids to take full advantage of what the Internet offers.

Teens have "been steeped in high technology to such a degree that it all but blends into the landscape. They've never known a world without touch-tone phones, VCRs, microwaves, compact discs, personal computers and the Internet. On its own, technology doesn't particularly excite them" (Wellner, 1999: 42–48).

1. Just having the Internet isn't enough. It is nothing special. In fact, it is assumed. Thus, our learning curve needs to rise. Continuous

training is the norm. If it can't be done in the classroom, there are hundreds of "online" classes or e-mail-based tutorials. There are hundreds of books, thousands of magazine articles, and endless Web pages giving how-to instructions on all aspects of computer and Internet use. We can't know everything, but most of us need to know a lot more than typing a word or phrase into a search engine's window and hoping for the best.

2. That said, realize that the ability to chat, build a Web page, or even hack into a Web page have little to do with the ability for teens to find information using the Internet. Work with the school librarians to develop a broad-based instruction plan for the teens in the community. Teach basic information problem solving, the "ins and outs" of a few of the best search engines, and above all teach about evaluating information.

3. Increase Internet capacity. Libraries are not spending enough on technology for teens. Consider Internet-only appliances, free Internet services like Zap Me, or any other alternative to increase capacity. If planning a new branch library, do we start with the "usual" number of terminals? What if instead we increased it five or ten times? The Internet *is* how students want and expect information resources to be delivered. That is what libraries are really about: providing access for information delivery. We are not in the book business, we are in the connecting-people-to-information business. If the primary information delivery vehicle is the Internet, then let's not merely accept that, but embrace it and plan our services around that fact. The main decision librarians serving teens should be confronting isn't about which books to buy, but rather which information appliance best meets our needs. YA librarians need to get on the automation committees, get on the Internet collection development work teams, and become the leaders in this rethinking of how we deliver services. The service remains the same, the tools are changing; just as we moved from hand writing card catalogs to typing them to buying cards for the catalog, then to fiche catalogs, and on to automated catalogs; just as we moved from music on 78s, then brought in the 45s, moved them out for albums, tapes, and then moved to compact discs. The question is not whether or not we'll connect our customers with music they want—it is only how we connect our customers with music. Maybe the model we should be looking at now is more workstations that can handle music downloads from sites like MP3, or, litigation pending, Napster?

"The future of the Web will trend toward social interaction. When they're on the Web, just as in the real world, teens focus on social activities. In addition to using the Internet as a tool for information gathering, e-commerce and schoolwork, teens also view the Web as a means to keep in touch and interact with friends. This attitude can have great implications for Website design and software evolution" (Ebenkamp, 1999: 18–22).

1. If we ban chat or e-mail from our Internet terminal, we take away the number one reason teens want to use the Internet. Why is checking stock quotes any more necessary or "valued" than chatting? Look for methods to "manage" chat, such as time limits, chat-only computers, or some computers with no chat and only available for research, etc. But banning chat is banning many teens, especially teens who do not have computers at home.
2. Add interactivity to the library's Web page. Set up and promote interactive reference. Give it a brand name, a look, a logo, and then promote its use at schools and through signage in the library. Use forms teens may submit, e-mail, or even "librarian chat" to add the element teens are looking for on the Internet. Why not "video chat"? Investigate adding Web cams to selected terminals. Think about it: A teen gets stuck doing a search, then clicks on "talk to a librarian" and it opens up a two-way videoconference. This isn't *The Jetsons*, the technology is there to do this today, if we have the vision to make it happen.
3. Add chat as an element to after-school tutoring programs. Rather than asking volunteer tutors to come to the library to assist one group of teens, why not keep the tutors in a central place and allow kids in need of help to go online to get assistance. No, it is not the valued one-on-one, in-person interaction, but given the busy schedule and often-difficult transportation issues faced by many teens, this might be the way to go.

"A significant percentage of teens have their own Websites and many of them intend to start online businesses in the future. Half of teens surveyed felt that the Internet was not only a natural part of their future, but a critical component. In addition, teens who have their own Websites are on the leading edge of many online trends" (Ebenkamp, 1999: 18–22).

1. Get teens involved in building library Websites; in particular those aimed at teens. They know how to do this better than most of us.

They know what works and what doesn't. We can do the "librarian" part of collection development, such as choosing the links, but allow the teens to control the design, graphics, and architecture, as well as adding links they choose.

2. Form Web camps or computer clubs, in particular in neighborhoods where kids are less likely to have access to computers at home. Use free Web-hosting services like tripod.com, which provides templates and step-by-step instructions on Website creation. Work with after-school programs, such as 21st Century Schools or with youth-serving agencies to place these kids into jobs building Web pages. Visit *www.benton.org*, get informed, and then involved in the "digital divide" campaign that will provide funding streams for exactly these types of programs. If the Internet is going to be "the future," public libraries should try to get teens access to that future.

3. Work with teachers to have students design resource pages for particular assignments, similar to the Big6™ pages described in Chapter 11. Use this as an opportunity to teach information problem solving, Website evaluation, and other skills kids will need to be informed and prepared to deal effectively in the information economy. For example, I worked with a group of middle school students to develop, design, and then post a Web page on Cinco de Mayo. Using the Big6™ model, the middle schoolers created Web pages about various aspects of traditions associated with this holiday. Each page was brief, factual, and well sourced. Rather than merely handing in a paper on the subject, the students had a chance to learn/practice a skill, as well as creating an information resource for others, as in essence they created an online bibliography with the "best" sites they used to create their pages. Total effort on the part of the public library: two hours to teach and two hours to review the pages before posting them.

REACHING THE TEEN MARKET

"The teen market will grow twice as fast as the overall population through 2010, topping off at 35 million" (Heller, 1999: 34).

1. If you have not done so already, make sure everyone knows this essential fact—the director, the board, the friends, the staff. The agenda to serve teens has nothing to do with "good feelings" but rather cold, hard numbers; there are going to be lots of teens very soon.

2. Make sure that this number is at hand when looking at library budgets. To successfully respond to this coming wave of teenagers, library budgets MUST focus more resources into materials and services for teenagers. The costs of not doing so are enormous in terms of lost opportunities for the teens, the library, and the community.

3. Have a plan. Bring together folks from the youth-serving agencies, youth ministries, schools, and other groups that will also all "bear the brunt" of this age wave. Work toward community partnerships that empower teens and make the participating organizations stronger.

"About 95 percent of the nation's teens listen to FM radio, averaging more than ten hours each week. Especially in small towns, radio connects local teenagers, informing them of coming events such as concerts, sports, school events, and so on. Radio also makes celebrities out of local disc jockeys. And, in most markets, there are typically a few strong teen stations, allowing advertisers to efficiently reach large numbers of teens" (Zollo, 1999: 35–36).

1. Put down this book, go over to the phone book and make a list of the stations in your community. Start listening and determine which station best reaches the teen market that you want to reach. Music/radio is very fragmented; kids who listen to rap don't normally also listen to bubblegum pop. Better yet, start asking the kids you want to reach what station they listen to most.

2. Contact the station with a very concrete proposal. Not "let's work together" but have something in mind that they can "own" and put their brand name on— the teen summer reading program, the after-school program, Teen Read Week programs, etc. Come with hard information about how many kids you think you can reach. Ask the station to sign on as the official media sponsor for the program.

3. Once a relationship has been built, try to get a PSA created and aired about the library, perhaps about reference services, during after-school and evening hours. Even better, if you are up to it, partner with the station in contests, remotes, or other promotions.

"Teens report that they don't want to be preached to or patronized; you have to reach them in new, creative ways" (Silverman, 1998: 8+).

1. Let's review how we do library instruction. Is there too much preaching? Instruction should be cooperative in nature, often one-on-one. Learn what the teen already knows, and then build upon on it.
2. Unhinge the creativity of the people who work in libraries. Most people who work with kids can, if given the chance, develop creative solutions. The first step is to rid us of the old ways and embrace change rather than resisting it. Resistance, while not futile, is counterproductive to the organization and to the individual. Consider if we had nothing, what would we build? If we just started trying to serve teens in libraries, what would we do now?
3. New creative ways could means lots of things, but look at them in terms of the collection. Does what we do still work? Does a collection full of hardback novels, well-reviewed nonfiction, and shelf upon shelf of reference materials work best? Should we even buy reference books? What information do the majority of reference books we have used for years with kids for homework have that can not be found via the Internet on free or subscription databases? If we clear out all those reference books, what are we going to do with the space? Fill it with more ALA best books, or maybe with graphic novels, true crime paperbacks, magazines and locally produced zines, DVDs, circulating CD-ROMs, etc.

"While older teens dislike the term 'teen' or even 'teenager,' 'tweens' (eight to fourteen year olds) like being called teens. . . . Marketing products with 'teen' in the name should focus on the tween market rather than the 14–and-older market. The popularity of *Seventeen* magazine with pre-teens and young teens is a classic example of aspirational consumerism—actual 17–year-olds read adult women's magazines" ("Teen Consumer Brand Loyalty . . . ," 1999: 1+).

1. Set up young adult areas that cater to the interests and needs of older teenagers. Fill them with the gritty fiction, college and career guides, and cutting-edge adult fiction and nonfiction. Put them literally "on the edge" of our YA areas and promote their use to older teenagers.
2. Don't get hung up on labels—they can turn off as well as on. I'll say it again, the best YA area doesn't need a sign that says "YA" or "teen"—it should be obvious from the racks of magazines, the shelves of Cliff Notes and classics, and the whole feeling that this is where kids, from ten to twenty, belong.

3. Really look hard at the "tween" market. Read the cover story *Newsweek* called "tweens" and think of the implications for your library and the services you provide to this segment of the youth market (Kantrowitz, 1999: 62–72). Work cooperatively with children's librarians and elementary school librarians to expand programming options to this group. If you "reach" this group now and turn them into customers, chances are they will remain loyal customers for years (and potentially for generations) to come.

"One mall even employs teen consumers to be part of the 'style squad' to give detailed feedback on everything from how retailers can better arrange displays and position fashions to the approach that salespeople should take to become more teen-friendly" (Buss, 1999: 16).

1. The benefit of teen participation is no secret. Using them as a focus group might only be a start. Hire or recruit as volunteers a cadre of kids to be secret shoppers. Provide them with some of the checklists of behaviors to look for (approachable, friendly, etc.), give them reference or readers' advisory questions to ask in person, over the phone, or via e-mail, and then have them "rate" their responses. Do we provide quality customer service to teens? Only they can tell us and this is the best way to gather that information.
2. A library should produce nothing, no booklist or flyer or sign, for teens without teens passing judgment over it. Set up a Teen Editorial Board—again, formally or informally. Maybe they meet once a week, or maybe it is a group of three kids you send e-mail attachments to before sending things to press.
3. Bring in teens to give your YA area a makeover. With a little bit of money, they could probably do a lot to make the YA area more customer friendly, from changing the arrangement of materials to the color scheme to the furniture arrangement. Involve a teen group in helping to plan YA areas in new buildings or in ones to be renovated.

"There has been a 'remarkable growth of teen-oriented stores' filling up shopping malls" (Buss, 1999: 16).

1. The retail community is taking notice of teens and setting aside space for them; libraries should follow the trend. These teen-focused businesses and products all provide potential partners for reaching teens through media or through programming.

2. Meet the managers of these stores and ask about training. What special training do they offer their customer service staff in serving teens?

3. Chances are good that the manager's answer to the question about special training will be, "not much," since the majority of customer service staff working after school, evenings, and weekends are other teens. Libraries *must* follow suit and employ more teens to work in our libraries, and not just to shelve books. We could easily recruit, train, and employ a cadre of teens to be out on the public floor working with other teens. They have more credibility and perhaps even more of the necessary skills. Face it—some teens know more than we do about finding information on the Internet. The "knowledge power" we had is gone. We might once have been the only ones who knew what was in those specialized reference books. But every kid who has grown up on the Net knows what is inside those search engines just as well as we do, if not better. Why are we not taking advantage of this knowledge base? More important, however, is the long-term survival of our profession. With the impending retirement of the Baby Boomers in the offing and the tendency for what used to be library schools to turn out people who would rather work just about any place but a library, we need to start recruiting for this profession today. One solid way to do that is to employ teens and "turn them on" to what we do. If we train them, empower them, and encourage them, they might just be ready to replace us.

"Teens expect unflagging customer service, speed-of-light e-commerce, just-in-time delivery, generous return policies, rock solid guarantees, and deep discounts. Simply put, they're the toughest, most demanding, and most fickle customers in the world" (Hoffman, 1999: 33–36).

1. Let's survey these customers on a regular basis. If we are going to make a commitment to improving service, let's establish benchmarks to determine where we are. Don't have time? See if a local college has students looking for internships or fieldwork in the fields of marketing and/or educational research. Let them do the work, gain the experience, and we can reap the benefits of the information they gather.

2. Do libraries do any of these things well? Do we deliver services at the speed of light or even just in time? Do we make guarantees or

give discounts? No, but can we? Why couldn't the public library set up a daily delivery service with high schools? Working with the school librarian, you put the library's Web-based catalog as the first link or even the homepage for each computer. Kids search the catalog, find what they want, and then ask for it to be delivered to the school library for pick up. Or maybe we mail it to their house and put the "fee" for the service on their account to be paid the next time they come in the building? Maybe we join with school library networks that have magazine fax services to deliver articles to schools. The school could eat the cost or pass it on to the student. There are no reasons in terms of technology these things can't be done. They can be done and they should be done if we break away from the model that requires teens to find transportation, find a parking spot, find a time when we are open, and then find the information they need. Instead, they can sit at home or in front of their school library computer, point and click, and get delivery of information "just in time" (OK, it won't work for the night before—except for 24/7 subscription databases).

3. Can we offer discounts? Library policies vary, but of course we can. We could offer "fine vouchers" as summer reading incentives. We could have amnesty days that generate good press—how about one over the holiday where fines could be paid by donating canned goods to the poor? How about an amnesty day at individual schools with rewards for the schools that collect the most over-due books? How about letting teens work off their fines through volunteering? How about no printing charges for kids in after-school programs? How about free parking for teens who attend a library instruction program? How about "frequent shoppers" cards where after ten check outs there is some value added?

These are just a few examples of the types of ideas generated in the business community to reach the teen market. Make it a point to search your periodical databases and look for articles like these. Make it a point to travel to the mall every now and then just to observe. Make a point to ask managers at teen-friendly stores like the Gap to talk with you or maybe even train your staff. And finally, make it a point to realize that the teen "market" is huge, but also fragmented. Every possible demographic marker, in addition to interests, library use, and attitudes about reading and libraries can divide the market. We appeal to the broad middle of the market, doing our best to move the majority of kids our way. But once they are customers, stop thinking of them as "market seg-

ments" and instead remember that they are the people on the other side
of the customer service relationship.

REFERENCES

Buss, Dale. 1999. "Teen Nation." *Brandmarketing* 6, no. 11 (November): 16.

Cogner, Peggy. 1999. "Marketing to Today's Kid." *Cable World* 11, no. 44 (November 1): 2a+.

Ebenkamp, Becky. 1999. "Cyber Teens Get Social." *Brandweek* 40, no. 33 (September 6): 18–22.

Heller, Laura. 1999. "The Customer Connection: Teen Talk, 13 to 19 Years." *Discount Store News* 38, no. 20 (October 25): 34.

Hoffman, Mike. 1999. "Searching for the Mountain of Youth." *Inc* 21, no. 18 (December): 33–36.

Kantrowitz, Barbara. 1999. "The Truth About Tweens." *Newsweek* 134 (October 18): 62–72.

Silverman, Dick. 1998. "Malls Have That Teen Spirit Again." *DNR* 28, no. 56, (May 11): 8+.

"Teen Consumer Brand Loyalty Varies According to Product Category." 1999. *Youth Markets Alert* 11, no. 7 (1999): 1+.

"Tracking Teens." 1999. *Women's Wear Daily Merchandising Juniors Supplement* (May): 6+.

Wellner, Alison. 1999. "Get Ready for Generation Next." *Training* 36, no. 2 (February): 42–48.

Zollo, Peter. 1999. "Not Quite the TV Generation." *American Demographics* 21, no. 5 (May): 35–36.

Chapter 9

Twenty Steps to Customer Service Success

Patrick Jones

What can you do today to improve customer service? You are ready to make changes in your customer attitudes and behaviors, but what about the larger organization? In a perfect world, customer service would really be the lifeblood of a public library, not just some nice words written in a mission statement. But in order to create raving fans, it is not enough for one or two people to change the organization needs to embrace customer service. Your part is to be a model, a champion, maybe even a customer service "rebel" in your library. Start the fire, start climbing those golden stairs toward creating a solid base of satisfied teen customers.

The following list represents twenty steps to customer service success. It is adapted from a list in *Beyond Customer Service: Keeping Customer for Life* by Richard Gerson (1994: 51-64) on "ways to keep your customers for life." Consider each step and how it might improve customer service in your library.

Step One: Have a service vision. This is the first step in the raving fans approach: Your vision should be based on your experiences as a 14 year old. Recall how you were treated or how you should have been served. Turn yesterday's memories (whether positive or negative) into developing today's vision of excellent customer service.

Step Two: Support employee training. Joanne M. Bessler's excellent *Putting Service into Library Staff Training: A Patron-Centered Guide*

(1994) provides an outstanding overview of how to train staff to provide service, while my own *Connecting Young Adults and Libraries* (1998) is loaded with training exercises directed at creating staff who are prepared, skilled, and empowered to work with teens. The key element, however, is having real training that starts with an orientation session that speaks to the values of customer service, the value of the customer, and finally to the value that the organization places on customer service. If library orientations for customer service merely mention, but don't clearly focus on, customer service, then new employees will realize that the organization's commitment to customer service isn't real, just more lip service. The more time spent training and preparing staff to provide optimal service, the more clearly customers and staff alike will recognize the high level of importance placed on customer service. If we only spend five minutes reading a "service statement" then we have shown our real commitment, or lack thereof, to training for real service. Some examples of service training for new employees should include the following key elements: writing a personal service pledge; shadowing the best people on the staff; shadowing patrons and talking with them after receiving service; doing role play related to problem solving with other staff; one-on-one coaching; meeting key support staff that support the customer service function; reading titles such as *The Service Edge* (Zemke, 1989); training in listening skills; and, finally, basic training in YA psychology in order to understand and appreciate the customer.

Step Three: Promote the service program through marketing. There is no sense doing good work if people don't know about it. Use Teen Read Week or some other "celebration" to kick off the program. Give it a brand name and develop a marketing program as if you were introducing a new service (which in fact, you just might be). Consider one- to three-word slogan/signs, buttons or stickers, or other ways to let people know the essential concept.

Step Four: Reward loyalty. Bookstores do it, why can't we set up reward programs for regular patrons? Sure the reward can't be a discount (or could it?), but find something to say to the kids who come in every day, who check out the most books. In a sense we do *do* this when we set up a YA summer reading program that rewards loyalty of our current users with prizes. Look for other opportunities to involve and reward frequent customers.

Step Five: Expect what you expect. List the qualities you expect from others serving young adults, such as being approachable and nonjudgmental. Highlight the most important ones and post them. People can't meet your expectations (nor can you meet your own) if you are not perfectly clear on what those expectations are.

Step Six: Trade jobs. Let someone else walk in the YA's shoes for a while.

Step Seven: Cross train. Avail yourself to inservice opportunities such as the "training the trainer" workshops offered by YALSA to learn even more ways to take this message of "moment of truth" customer service to others in your system, your region, and your state. Spread the word to all library employees. Customer service "happens" more at the circulation desk than at the reference desk: just compare the number of transactions that occur at each location.

Step Eight: Handle complaints properly. Teens will rarely complain, which is too bad because a patron complaint will result in more action and improvement than a training plan.

Step Nine: Train your employees to do it right the first time. The cost of noncompliance is huge; not just for the YA patron who never comes back, but also for the one who is persistent and gets in line time and time again to get service.

Step Ten: Beg for customer feedback. In addition to comment cards, look for other ways to gather feedback. Again, either low-tech (suggestion boxes) or high tech (Web page form submissions) will work. Put customer comment cards in kid's hands; distribute them at school visits, and reward those who take the time to turn them in. Do surveys, focus groups, and interviews—anything it takes. On surveys, make it simple: What one thing could we do better? What one thing do we do right? See the longer sample teen customer survey in Figure 9.1.

Step Eleven: Identify customer values, beliefs, and standards. Ask teens to rank valuable services in order of importance. Maybe they think we do after-school programs well, but it is not important to them, while they may think we stink at Internet access, which is their number one priority. Teens value speed and respect; those should be our values.

Step Twelve: Get employee ideas. Turn the staff loose in coming up with creative solutions. Release folks from the daily grind of their job and the urge to complain by allowing them to expand their jobs/minds/ imaginations and seek solutions. Employee contests, suggestion plans, and the like should also be considered.

Step Thirteen: Underpromise and overdeliver. This is hard to fulfill because it is *so* easy to overpromise because we firmly believe in what we do. But it does make more sense to set expectations a little lower and then "wow!" them by exceeding their expectations. This could take many forms, such as telling a patron how long it might take to get a book through interlibrary loan and then surprising them by getting the book sooner than expected.

Step Fourteen: Understand that high touch is more important than high tech. If anything, all this technology should make us more customer-service orientated, especially to teens. As we all know, searching the Internet or even databases such as Electric Library is *not* always easy, so pointing to a computer and saying "good luck" won't cut it for most of our young adult customers. They won't ask for help in many cases, so do a search with them, talking it out, and be sure not to leave them until they have what they need in hand.

Step Fifteen: Ask customers what they want. And ask them again and again and again.

Step Sixteen: Know the cost of losing a customer. This is a simple training technique. Use the remembrance exercise from the Prelude to help other staff think about their own moments of truth. Were they library users, and if not, why not? The research tells us that kids who "turn off" from reading and libraries are very unlikely to return. The teen years are, in many cases, where many people set patterns and habits for life. So let's do our best to create future adult library users today by treating our young adult customers with the respect they need and deserve.

Step Seventeen: Find, nurture, and display customer service champions. Make sure you share these success stories in some way. Set up a "service hall of fame" bulletin board, route positive YA customer comments, and praise, praise, praise.

Step Eighteen: Know that rapport is the key to successful communication. You don't need to speak slanguage or street lingo to relate to teens; you just need to develop rapport. Rapport is based on understanding, but mostly on respect. Respect them and they will respond in kind.

Step Nineteen: Promote your customers. Consider, especially with after-school programs, having a "student of the month" or something of that nature to promote kids using the library not only to other kids, but

Figure 9–1   Sample teen customer survey

Hennepin County Teen User Survey

Hennepin County Library wants to improve how it serves teens. We are gathering information to learn what we can do better. Please take a minute to help us help you–

What grade are you in? (circle one)

7   8   9   10   11   12

What school do you attend?

What Library do you most visit?

How often do you use the Library? (check one)

[ ]Every day   [ ]Every week   [ ]Every month   [ ]Once or twice a year   [ ]Never

Pick a number from the scale to describe why you use the Library to do each of the items listed below. [1 = frequently, 2 = sometimes, 3 = seldom, 4 – never]

[ ]Use the catalog, databases, or Teen Web Page	[ ]Checkout materials to use for homework	[ ]Checkout materials to read for fun	[ ]Checkout materials to read for information	[ ]Checkout music tapes or CDs
[ ]Access the Internet	[ ]Checkout videotapes	[ ]Meet and talk with friends	[ ]Attend a library event	[ ]Study
[ ]Other:				

If you don't often use the Library, what is the primary reason? (check one)

[ ]Unable to get to the library	[ ]Not enough time	[ ]Nothing at the library interests me	[ ]Don't need it	[ ]Do research/find reading material elsewhere	[ ]Not sure what the library has to offer me
[ ] Other:					

What three things could the Hennepin County Library do better in serving teens? Select three [1 = top choice, 2 = 2nd choice, 3 = 3rd choice]

[ ]Set up a youth advisory group	[ ]More magazines	[ ]Create after-school tutoring program	[ ]More study space for teens
[ ]Keep the Library open later	[ ]More books for school work	[ ]Promote what the Library offers better	[ ]More staff to work with teens
[ ]Create a teen summer reading program	[ ]More books to read for pleasure (what kind?)	[ ]Have more services available on the Web	[ ]More events (what kind?)
[ ]Other:			
[ ]Other:			
[ ]Other:			

OPTIONAL: May we contact you to gather more information? *Your name, address, and telephone number are private. It is available only to appropriate library staff in support of library service.*

Name	Phone	E-mail

EXERCISE: The Chinese Menu

Look over the list of twenty steps to keep customers for life. Now, make three lists of your own. On the A-list, write down the top five that most appeal to you as a customer. On the B-list, write down the five that would most appeal to the library director/board. On the C-list, write down the five that would most appeal to teens. What, if any, are the common themes? Knowing you can't do all of them, choose some from the A-list, some from the B-list, but mostly from the C-list.

---

also to staff. Take pictures of kids using the library and try to get pics of groups—clubs, sports teams, and class councils—holding up library cards. Let kids do "my favorite books" displays or their own booklists.

Step Twenty: Create a customer council. Do this today. Set up a teen advisory board from patrons by working with a school or in any other fashion. In addition to planning programs and the like, you really want them—as library customers—to give you feedback and input on how you are doing.

REFERENCES

Bessler, Joanne. 1994. *Putting Service into Library Staff Training: A Patron-Centered Guide.* Chicago: American Library Association.

Gerson, Richard. 1994. *Beyond Customer Service.* Menlo Park, CA: Crisp Publications.

Jones, Patrick. 1998. *Connecting Young Adults and Libraries: A How-To-Do-It Manual.* Second edition. New York: Neal-Schuman.

Zemke, Ron, and Dick Schaaf. 1989. *The Service Edge: 101 Companies That Profit From Customer Care.* New York: Penguin.

Chapter 10

Listen to Your Customers: Buy More Magazines

Patrick Jones

The Houston Public Library conducted a reading interest survey as part of its Teen Read celebration in 1998. The format of choice was not books or comic books, but magazines. This should come as no surprise given what we know about YA life—the need for quick bursts of information about what is *now*—supports buying more magazines. Finally, simply creating a large, eclectic magazine collection is a wonderful demonstration of the customer service mantra: the customer knows best.

Just as retailers are responding to the coming teenage wave, so are magazine publishers with a variety of new titles, many of them spin-offs of familiar adult standards (*Teen People, Cosmo Girl*, etc.). The titles in the following list were selected to demonstrate the wide variety of magazines available that may be of special interest to young adults. It includes new titles such as those listed above, but you won't find *Teen, Seventeen, YM, Boys Life*, or any of those "usual suspects" here: this list assumes you already get those magazines. Not listed here either are selection tools, although anyone doing YA collection development should subscribe to *The Voice of Youth Advocates* as well as *Yahoo Life*. Before getting to the list, let's look at some of the movements in the marketplace.

While several of the new titles are aimed at teenage girls, others are trying to capture the boy market, and some are reaching toward the growing Hispanic market. Publishers are hoping to get these groups to develop the same "attachments" to magazines that girls have developed over the years. Writing in *Mediaweek*, Jeff Gremillion notes "Advertisers are hungry to find efficient, large-scale means to reach impression-able teens who have yet to establish brand loyalties. Boys are also known to have strong attachments to the magazines they read, and their gener-ous pass-along tendencies mean there are several readers for every single subscriber or newsstand buyer" (Gremillion, 1999: 40).

The dilemma for magazine publishers is similar to those faced by li-braries: What to do with not just *Rolling Stone* and *Spin*, but also with titles like *Maxim* and *Details* which have a strong teen appeal but are really geared to the 20–28 set? Gremillion writes that "the few mass titles are geared to adults, and too strong an association with teenagers could jeopardize lucrative alcohol and tobacco advertising. *Sports Illustrated, Spin,* and *Rolling Stone* all say they do not market to anyone younger than 18" (Gremillion, 1999: 40). The route most marketers have taken to get to boys then is not only those titles mentioned, but also to adver-tise in more "friendly" titles like *Nintendo Power* or specific sports titles. That makes sense with the continued fragmentation of teen culture. Christina Merrill writes in *American Demographics*, that in contrast to "targeting teens with a one-size-fits-all approach, her division prefers to market tactically to certain teen subgroups" (1999: 27). Merrill quotes a senior executive in media who goes so far as to say, "There is no such thing as a teen category for magazines. . . . there is a teen girl category, and then you've got the boys" (1999: 27). If boys read anything, it's titles that reflect their interest in sports, computer games, and music.

The teen girl category has upstarts such as *Twist* and, even more pow-erful, *Cosmo Girl*. Writing in *Folio*, Vira Mamchur Schwartz observes about the new title that if you, "Take away the sex, substitute 'backpack' for 'bedside' astrologer, use younger fashions and models, include Hollywood's younger hunks (and throw in some stickers of the stars), focus on giving girls confidence to be themselves, have lots of contest giveaways—and you have *CosmoGirl!*" (1999: 69–70). While *Cosmo Girl* hopes to reach an already established audience by having a killer brand, an even more exciting development are the new magazines, *Latina* and *Latin Girl*. After the demise of *YSB* (*Young Sisters and Brothers*), there was little cultural/racial/ethnic diversity in the teen mass-market maga-zine field until these new titles recently appeared. Armed with market research data about the growing number of Hispanic teens and their pro-digious spending habits, Micromedia Inc. of Miami launched *Latin Girl* in the spring of 1999. Rachel Weissman in *American Demographics* quotes the publisher of *Latin Girl* as saying "We conducted surveys with 600 girls in the three major Hispanic markets: Los Angeles, New York, and Miami . . . we spoke by phone with girls of different origins, some U.S.-born and some immigrants, all attending English-speaking schools" (1999: 37). The research found that while language didn't present a problem with reading a magazine like *Seventeen*, interviewees said such magazines didn't reflect their physical appearance and lifestyle. Weissman notes that *"Latin Girl* hopes to fill that void" (1999: 37).

The other two big explosions are in the area of fanzines, such as *Bop*. As each new generation runs its heroes up the pop charts, marketing initiatives and a boom market for fanzines now are sure to follow. For libraries, these titles present the usual problems of potential theft and vandalism, but also the new problem of keeping up with all the special supplements. Almost every magazine puts out "special editions" about individual stars, so make sure your magazine vendor can supply these. The other huge area of increase is professional wrestling magazines There are three main types of magazines: the first are those published by the companies themselves: WWF, WCW, and ECW. The WWF is nationally popular, while WCW still has its base in the south. ECW is very popular in the northeast, although the ratings of its spotlight show on TNN pull a 1.1 rating, while WWF kills on Monday nights with ratings in the 7s, making WWF Raw the highest rated show on cable. The WWF also publishes the *Raw* magazine; the title gives away the content. While certainly not "pornographic," the focus here is normally pictorials of the women wrestlers/valets/managers. The second type of magazine are the so-called Apter magazines published by G.C. London. The "oldest" (I recall reading *The Wrestler* when I was a teenager) cover all the federations, with emphasis on the big three. The titles are totally interchangeable: *Inside Wrestling* is no more "inside" than *Pro Wrestling Illustrated* is more "illustrated." Finally, the new breed of magazine is best represented by *WOW*—easily the best of the bunch; in fact, it has won some newsstand awards. With lots of inside stuff for the smart fans, this is a good cross between the "dirt sheets" like *Pro Wrestling Torch, (www.pwtorch.com)* and *Wrestling Observer, (www. wrestlingobserver.com)* and the more mainstream publications. While not every YA is a wrestling fan, there is no denying the popularity of this "sports entertainment" and of the magazines. One of my own reasons for *not* using my public library as a teen was simply because they didn't get wrestling magazines. If they had, I would have visited the library every week.

The following is a list of magazines with current appeal to a broad range of young adults. Look the list over and consider adding them to your collection as dictated by the interests of your YA customers.

All About You	*Teen's* little cousin aimed at middle school girls. Still catching on.
American Cheerleader	A slick glossy monthly magazine for those who are cheerleaders, and even more for those who want to become one.
American Girl	Aimed at very young teens/older elementary, this publication from Pleasant Company keeps the same theme and spirit of "wholesomeness" found in the American Girl books. It is contemporary in its look more so than its outlook. Filled with stories, games, party plans, sports tips, contests, and more.
Analog Science Fiction	An oldie but goodie featuring science fiction short stories by current authors, science fact articles, and book reviews.
Alternative Press	While *Rolling Stone* covers mainstream music and twenty-something's culture/concerns, *Alternative Press* looks at the edges of music and taps into youth culture. Each monthly issue includes interviews with indie (independent) bands as well as established acts. The magazine targets fans of alternative, indie, ska, electronic, dub, industrial, punk, techno, underground, rock, ambient, experimental, and other musical genres.
Archaeology's Dig	An interesting new bimonthly magazine backed by Disney brings the fascination and the fun of archaeology to preteens. Taking examples of science in popular culture, like the movie *The Mummy*, this heavily illustrated periodical hopes to link kids' interest in science-based fiction with the facts. Aimed primarily at younger teens, there are lots of illustrations. With engaging text, photographs, games, projects, and comics, *Dig* uncovers mummies, discoveries, ancient civilizations, and more.
Asimov's Science Fiction	One of the leading science fiction and fantasy magazines. With submissions by both new talent and some of the leading names in science fiction, the magazine is a treasure for young fans

	of the fantastic and future worlds. Each issue features novellas and short stories, as well as book reviews, editorials, and other features.
Bike	For the hardcore biking enthusiast, this glossy title covers both mountain and urban biking. Loaded with photos, product reviews, and feature articles on all aspects of biking, this title claims to have "all the tools and information to keep readers on the cutting edge."
Biography	While the homework potential for this title can't be denied, *Biography* has a lot more going for it than simply as report fodder. A spin-off of the *Biography* series on the A&E Network, each issue includes portraits of superstars, special takes on the extraordinary acts of ordinary people, profiles of historical figures, and biography reviews. With the teen fascination with both celebrity and success, *Biography* offers more weight than *People* and snappier writing (and much better pictures) than *Current Biography*.
Blast	One of the more popular new fanzines to emerge in the Backstreet Boys era, the title says it all with a real blast of color, pin-ups, and focus on stars whose careers resemble comets: Did anyone say New Kids On the Block?
Blaze	A new magazine focusing on black entertainers, particularly in the music industry. Not as serious as *The Source* but one step up from most fanzines.
Blitz	A new football magazine loaded with action pictures and attitudes, from the same company that produces the basketball title *Slam*.
BMX Plus	With the onslaught of cable TV coverage of extreme sports, BMX bike racing has gained in popularity. One of the best of the lot, *BMX Plus* is loaded with articles about every aspect of BMX racing and is copiously illustrated with photos of bikes in action, normally in mid-air.

Bop	One of the stalwarts of teen fanzinedom, *Bop* has found new life with the most recent teen idol craze. Known for its "you focused" article style and even more for more loading every issue with posters to fit in any locker or on any notebook, *Bop* is the bible of the FM radio teen pop culture scene.
Box	Yet another magazine tying to knock *Thrasher* off the top of the skate heap by being more hip. Loaded with dazzling photography, information on events and equipment, interviews with top skaters, and stories from/by/about skaters, *Box* is one of the best in a crowded market.
Breakaway	From *Focus on the Family* comes a magazine aimed at teen guys. Featuring the usual suspects of sports and celebrities, coupled with "issues" like peer pressure, parents, dating, etc., this title represents a Christian/values-based perspective on teen life.
Brio	The companion to *Breakaway* for teen girls. Mixing fashion tips with faith-based articles, sure to be popular in many communities with large home-schooling populations.
Cicada	A bimonthly publication for young adults ages 14 and up. It offers high-quality fiction and poetry dealing with the issues of growing up, leaving the joys and pains of childhood behind, and becoming an adult. *Cicada* also encourages its teen readers to submit their own writing for publication.
Computer Gaming World	By the numbers, the top magazine for computer game players. Every issue is packed with in-depth reviews, winning secrets, sneak previews of the newest games, the latest updates on new technologies, and more to let readers get the most out of every minute they spend playing computer games.

Cosmo Girl	Long overdue is the *Cosmo* spin-off for teenagers. Subtitled "a magazine for real girls with real issues," the usual stuff is here, such as dating/guys, beauty, fashion, money, parents, school, health, and more. Each bimonthly issue has insider beauty and fashion secrets plus celebrity and runway fashion trends that readers can actually afford and find at local malls. There is also plenty of advice about situations at home, at school, and with friends.
Dragon	A tough call showing one of the challenges of magazine collection development. *Dragon* is hugely popular with kids who like fantasy role-playing games which, despite the emergence of so many computer games ripping off the basic concepts of D & D, still seem to be big with some kids. Those kids are often "fanatics" about the game and are likely to have this magazine anyway.
Electronic Gaming Monthly	This often-over-a-hundred-page-plus magazine provides readers the latest news, game reviews, and tips about the most exciting new games on Nintendo 64, PlayStation, Saturn, SuperNEW, Genesis, GameBoy, Game Gear, Jaguar, and Neo-Geo videogame systems.
Entertainment Weekly	The one magazine every public library serving teenagers needs to own. Loaded with regular features (the hot sheet among the best), this is truly the only magazine to cover all aspects of entertainment. A huge review section covers movies, TV, books, music, videos, and electronic media, not to mention quarterly Website round-ups. The covers more often than not feature the person or persons in the spotlight and the feature articles contain plenty of insight, sidebars, and photos.
ESPN	With the same mix of over-the-top reporting and irreverence which characterizes Sports Center and so much of ESPN's coverage, easily

	the best new magazine of the last few years. With a huge cable network to promote it as well as almost unprecedented coverage in all sports, *ESPN* is the *Sports Illustrated* for the cable generation. The editorial focus plays off the news and includes what will happen in sports and which match-ups and young players to watch. In addition, the magazine emphasizes the humor and fun of both mainstream and off-beat sports.
GamePro	Departments of note include "Buyers Beware," where readers ask technical questions and write about products that do not perform as advertised. In the "ProStrategy Section," readers can get the inside info they need to win with "The Fighter's Edge" and "S.W.A.T.Pro."
Girls' Life	Articles about clothes, make-up, boys, food, crafts, books, music, sports, getting along with parents, teachers, and friends, and much more are all packed into this upbeat publication. *Girls' Life* tried to thread the needle between the wholesomeness of magazines like *American Girl* and the more "sophisticated" approach of *Seventeen.*
Hit Parader	The old man of heavy metal keeps rocking along. The age of long-haired, heavily tattooed guitar heroes seems to have passed, but the energy and angst that drove them can still be found in plenty of indie and punk bands, which are now just as much the focus of *Hit Parader* as the latest exploits of Metallica or other heavy metal holdovers.
Inside NASCAR	The number one magazine for the number one fastest growing sport in the country. Covering the sport and personalities of NASCAR with plenty of great illustrations, *Inside NASCAR* is a fan's dream.
Inside Wrestling	One of the Apter family of magazines (named after long-time editor/photographer Bill Apter), there is little inside about *Inside Wrestling.* Instead,

	it covers the feuds and forays of the knights of the squared circle. Focusing heavily on the WWF and WCW, there is still coverage of smaller federations. Some dubious advertising and the traditional pictures of wrestlers whose bloody faces are described as "a crimson mask" make this a popular magazine among some kids and a cringe feast for most magazine check-in clerks.
Jump	The first teen fitness magazine. Like other fitness magazines, lots of advice-laden articles on nutrition, dieting, and exercising, as well as a generous amount of ads. But also a "lifestyle" magazine, which claims to "offer many ways for readers to achieve their own personal bests in life and love, inside and out." Published by the Weider group, who is the powerhouse in fitness and bodybuilding publishing.
Latin Girl	Long overdue, a title just for Latino teenagers. Nothing out of the ordinary, just the usual teen magazine fare offering tips on beauty, relationships, the latest styles, and more.
Latina	Just as *Glamour* and *Cosmo* are popular with older teenagers, this title will appeal to high school Hispanic girls. The monthly magazine features the latest information on fashion, beauty, health, fitness, and career opportunities, as well as profiles of today's newsmakers and celebrities.
Low Rider	Long a favorite because of the twin attractions of bikini-clad models standing next to souped-up cars, *Low Rider* presents several challenges. Wildly popular with teen males and especially Hispanics, keeping a copy on the shelf and intact make this wildly unpopular with many a librarian.
Men's Health Spin-Off	Planned for launch in early 2001, the Rodale Press (publisher of the very successful *Prevention* and *Men's Health* titles) is looking to break into the teen market.

Muse	The Smithsonian sponsors this bimonthly publication for 6-14 year olds. Featuring articles on space travel, foreign travel, computers, world history, and the look at the future, *Muse* brings the Smithsonian's collections, research, and expertise into focus in a glossy magazine.
National Enquirer	The king of tabloids. One of the most popular periodicals in the United States, yet almost always lacking from most public library collections. With its love of dish, its finger on the pulse of the "inquiring" public and backed with its own TV show, not to mention a horde of imitators, this is the best celebrity-rich scandal rag.
NBA Inside Stuff	Sponsored by the NBA, this title is loaded with player profiles and action photos as the league tries to generate interest in the post-Jordan, post-strike environment.
New Moon	Aimed at pre-teen and young teen girls, *New Moon* is a "new age" magazine for this set. *New Moon* is like *Teen Voices* in that it attempts to capture girls' interest by presenting alternative views before they are forever lost to the plastic land of *Teen/Seventeen/YM*, and the like. With girl editors ages 8 to 14 and girl contributors from all over the world, *New Moon* celebrates girls, explores the passage from girl to woman, and builds healthy resistance to gender inequities.
Nickelodeon	An award-winning entertainment magazine from the number one network for kids. It's packed with celebrity interviews, fascinating facts, comics, pull-outs, puzzles, and more.
Nintendo Power	Loaded, totally loaded, with game hints and previews, the bible for the Game Boy generation.
OneWorld	A new entry into a crowded field, with an emphasis on black entertainers. *OneWorld* features personal interviews and profiles and lots of news about music and film.

PC Gamer	One of the better gaming magazines. There is a lot of emphasis here on all sorts of games, not just one product line or format.
Premiere	A monthly magazine for movie junkies. *Premiere* takes readers behind the scenes of newly released and soon-to-be-released films. The magazine answers questions about the business and art of moviemaking and helps readers get a better understanding of the movie industry. *Premiere* also features interviews, profiles, and film commentary.
Pro Wrestling Illustrated	Another Apter magazine focusing on all wrestling federations. Featuring lots and lots of photos, this is one of the oldest and best in the crowded field of wrestling magazines.
Rap Pages	Mirroring the rawness and attitude of the music it covers, *Rap Pages* is filled with lyrics, profiles, and news.
Right On	One of the pre-rap magazines, there is a lot more emphasis on urban contemporary artists in this magazine than just rap artists.
Rolling Stone	Although no longer the "only game in town" the granddaddy of rock-and-roll magazines still leads the pack. Serving up the latest news in popular culture (there was even a cover story of professional wrestling), music, celebrities, and politics, *Rolling Stone* is still one of the most popular magazines read by teenagers; even if the "true" audience is twenty-somethings. After shaking off its love affair with dinosaur rock stars that the magazine grew up with in the 60s and 70s, and answering the challenge of more competition on the newsstand, *Rolling Stone* confirms for many what is hot and what is not. Plenty of music, film, and book reviews fill the text. Photos by some of the best photographers working today fill out the magazine as well as generate lots of heat with often controversial covers designed to catch attention by baring skin.

Science Fiction Age	A bimonthly publication that pushes the illustrations as much as the text. Aimed at the "serious" science fiction reader, each issue features fiction from the foremost authors with illustrations by today's leading artists. Book and movie reviews, interviews, and science facts supplement the "Alternative Media" section, which focuses on interactive technology, games, comics, collectibles, videos, and more.
Sci-Fi Entertainment	Yet another cable TV spin-off, this magazine reports on Sci-Fi Channel programming and displays beautiful photos, art, and movie stills. The magazine claims to be "leading source on all science fiction entertainment, covering movies, TV, online services, games, books, and more."
Sister 2 Sister	The only magazine aimed at African American teen girls, this title features both teen-like advice and issue columns with plenty of news of celebrities and "hunks."
Sixteen	One of the oldest and best of the fanzines.
Slam	The best basketball magazine on the market. Published eight times per year, it employs a hip tone in covering the NBA, ABA, high school level, and more. Each issue looks at the players behind the game and features the slam-dunk of the month.
Slap	Using skateboarding as the focus, this title tries to capture the essence of skate culture, street style, fashion, and new sounds.
Soccer Jr.	From interviews with star players to the latest U.S. and world soccer developments, *Soccer Jr.* is a well-rounded youth sports magazine. Its instructive articles cover the "moves and skills," the scoring tips, and the motivational secrets to help young players do their best. In addition, there are posters, games, and contests.
The Source	A serious rap magazine. Far different than a fanzine, *The Source* is the premier magazine of

	hip-hop with the most news, best reviews, and in-depth features on the issues, personalities, and controversies in the hip hop industry.
The Source Sports	Claiming to be "the voice of the new generation of athletes reared on hip-hop music and culture," this new title takes the hard edge of its parent magazine and applies it the world of sport. *The Source Sports* transcends the boundaries of traditional sports coverage, providing insight into the issues and athletes relevant to sports fans.
Spin	A magazine, which in the middle of the AIDS crisis included a condom in one issue, *Spin* remains the "bad boy" of the music scene. *Spin* focuses on the progressive music scene but also covers politics and pop culture.
Starlog	Perhaps the best of the various science fiction and fantasy magazines on the market. The *Starlog* brand name is a powerful magazine and they market a variety of spin-offs and special issues. Keeping to its base of *Star Trek/Star Wars* fans, *Starlog* looks at everything in the sci-fi industry.
SuperOnda	Published by Santa Barbara, California-based Hispanic Business magazine, this new title targets 16-22-year-olds. The magazine has a unique focus, looking at success in a career rather than on a date. The publisher believes that "Young readers of that age are at an impressionable stage when they're making important decisions, both about education and future career choices. The underlying concept is to provide readers with information in the economic sphere and about professions, to permit Hispanics to compete more effectively in today's market place."
Super Teen	Another fanzine; no better or worse than any others.
Talk	If the title alone wasn't a draw for teens, the heavy celebrity interviews and great covers will

	draw older teens to this title who want more than snippets found in *Entertainment Weekly* or *People*.
Teen Beat	See *Super Teen* above.
Teen en espanol	This Spanish-language version of *People* is a must for most urban public libraries, as well as others with a large Hispanic/Latino population.
Teen Machine	Yet another fanzine.
Teen Newsweek	Although mainly intended for the school audience, this magazine might be of interest to public libraries. An example of classic media synergy: *Newsweek* provides the content while the *Weekly Reader*, which has published its scholastic current-events magazine since 1928, handles production and distribution.
Teen People	This new kid on the block came out at the right time. Riding the crest of the "new wave" of teenagers coupled with the dramatic increase in popularity of all things teen in the music, TV, and movies, *Teen People* also happens to be very, very well done.
Teen Voices	An alliterative to *Teen* and that ilk, *Teen Voices* aims to challenge the mainstream media's image of girls by providing an intelligent alternative packed with original writing, poetry, and artwork. Like the late great *Sassy, Teen Voices* wants to "be its readers" and be the authentic voice for teen girls who reject the glossy world offered by *YM*. *Teen Voices* encourages readers to write articles on self-esteem, racism, sexism, feminism, popular culture, health, and other issues important to them.
Tiger Beat	It has been around at least since the days of the Monkees and for good reason: No magazine better catapults and exploits the hunk or cutie of the month like *Tiger Beat*.
Transworld Skateboarding	One of the oldest skating magazines, *Transworld* is a tamer version of *Thrasher*.

TV Guide	According to findings from the Teenage Research Institutes' spring 1999 survey, the only magazine that made the top-five list of both boys and girls was *TV Guide*, which placed third for guys and fifth for girls.
Twist	Another entry into the crowded girl magazine market. Mixing the column-heavy ("Guy Confession") and quiz-happy style ("Are You Too Hard on Yourself?") of girl magazines with the silliness of teen fanzines ("All About Andrew: We caught up with Andrew Keegan and discovered 10 things you'll love about him!"), *Twist* is a tweener for those moving out of thinking about Backstreet Boys and into going out with boys.
Upfront	A joint venture between the *New York Times* and Scholastic, this weekly title is aimed at high school kids with about 40 pages of content derived from stories from the *Times* but revised for the teen audience and with updates on a Website. According to the press kit, the magazine will "give high school-age readers general news with the *Times*' sophistication."
Us Weekly	The one-time monthly is ready to take *People* head-on by aiming at the 18-35 year old market on a weekly basis. With a new emphasis on fashion, as well as more musical coverage (after all, Jann Wenner, *Rolling Stone* founder, owns the magazine), this is a title every library will want to add for older YAs.
Vibe	More than just a music magazine, *Vibe* also covers the latest in movie, fashion, politics, sports, and technology. While focusing on hip-hop, *Vibe* covers all genres of urban music and lifestyle in its attempt to be the *Rolling Stone* for black culture.
Weekly World News	The very definition of camp. Loaded with one outrageous story after another, all of them seemingly variations of the same themes of "bat

	child found in cave," *Weekly World News* remains the hip tabloid.
Word Up	One of the oldest rap fanzines, *Word Up* remains a strong publication that looks at all variations of hip-hop with profiles, interviews, and lots (and lots) of photos.
WOW	One of the first of the new breed of professional wrestling magazine that occasionally really does "tell it like it is." While there is still the normal focus on stars, feuds, and matches, *WOW* looks "behind the ring" and examines the politics, intrigue, and issues behind the sport. Often breaking "kayfabe" (that is, admitting that wrestling is not true sport) brings some of the sensibility of the underground newsletter niche to the newsstand coupled with some of the best photographers. A great package and easily the best wrestling magazine available.
WWF	The official magazine from the World Wrestling Federation advances the storylines on its ratings-winning *Raw* and *Smackdown* shows, provides recaps of pay-per-views, and in-depth profiles of the talent. Lots of pictures of the "women of the WWF" to balance all the beefcake.
XXL	Easily the best of the new rap magazines, which focus on the entire street culture and not just the hottest bands or recordings.

Probably no public library could afford to purchase all of these magazines, unless it reflected a *huge* change in collection development strategies. Instead, this list presents a broad range of options that you should consider in terms of the demographics and interests of the teens in your community. Yes, magazines represent only one type of periodical literature popular with teens. Teens also read newspapers. Older teens favor the alternative or independent papers, not to mention zines which they or their friends may produce. While daily newspapers do not have the readership with teens they once did, there are sections, in particular the teen supplements, that are worth our attention. For example, the Houston Public Library teamed with the "Yo!" section of the *Houston Chronicle* to celebrate Teen Read Week in October 1999 with the entire supplement dedicated to reading, authors, and library programs.

Another way to attract YAs is to collect comic books and graphic novels. With the popularity of the *X-Men* movie in the summer of 2000, coupled with the continued popularity of stalwarts like *Batman* and *Superman*, not to mention "new" comics like *The Crow, Blade*, and *Spawn*, there is still a large audience (yes, mostly those pesky 12–year-old boys) for comics. Add the comic books based on computer games (such as *Tomb Raider*), TV shows (*X-Files*), and sports entertainment (WWF characters like the "Undertaker" have their own comics) to produce an outstanding collection-development opportunity that will help forge relationships with young readers, in particular male readers. Also consider Japanese anime, graphic science fiction novels, and graphic nonfiction like those produced by Dark Horse Comics (*The Big Book of Urban Legends*). Then there are always books on how to draw comics, CD-ROMs based on comics, and histories of comics. Development of these areas of the collection offer many programming opportunities, from the huge animation festival hosted by Los Angeles Public Library to the smallest comic book swap held in any public library's meeting room.

Collecting magazines, comics, and related products sends a clear message. The message from every reading interest survey, as well as the DeWitt Wallace surveys, is that teens want us to select and provide access to magazines. Thus, magazines are not just collection development, they are public relations, they are marketing, and they are relationship builders. Magazines demonstrate to our customers something very simple, very basic, and thus very important: we hear you.

REFERENCES

Gremillion, Jeff. 1999. "Where the Boys Are." *Mediaweek* (February 1): 40.

Merrill, Christina. 1999. "Keeping Up with Teens." *American Demographics* (October): 27.

Schwartz, Vira Mamchur. 1999. "Cosmo Gets a Little Sister." *Folio: The Magazine for Magazine Management* (September 1): 69–70.

Weissman, Rachel. 1999. "Los Ninos Go Shopping." *American Demographics* (May): 37.

Chapter 11

Netting Pathfinders with the Big6™

Patrick Jones

"The Big6™ process helped me find information more efficiently, allowing me to find it quickly and in more depth, and with a wider range than my previous research attempts."
—11th-grade student Caroline Hetton

Every public library faces the exact same challenge: handling the hordes of kids, children, and teenagers looking for information for science fair reports, on conducting the experiments, and the "elusive" science beyond the experiment information. These are staples of public library reference life. Many libraries do proactive things such as set up special collections, develop pathfinders, and/or hold workshops for parents and students about how to complete these projects. Always challenging for librarians because of the lack of information students often have about the details of the assignment, including such things as the basic requirements, due date, etc., developing special collections for parents and students has perhaps been made even more challenging today by the plethora of information resources now available to students via the Internet, online magazine indices, and full-text articles. There are a large number of science fair Websites available but few are of high quality. Because many students lack sophisticated information retrieval skills, today's science fair participants seem to need more help than ever. Given that this is a common connection point between libraries and teens, it is time to bring some order to this chaos.

The science fair, however, is not the only mass assignment. There is the other fair (the history fair), the state history assignment, the African American history assignment, not to mention whatever "favorites" that hit your library's reference desk every year like clockwork, serving only to frustrate customer and librarian alike. Rather than reacting, the Houston Public Library took a proactive approach by developing Web pages specifically created for both the science fair project (*www.hpl.lib.tx.us/youth/science_fair_index*) and the history fair project (*www.hpl.lib.tx.us/youth/history_fair_index*). Creating these pages in cooperation and consultation with the media specialists from the major school district (Houston Independent School District, which has over 250,000 students in 290 schools), the purpose of these Web pages is two-fold:

1. To save time, effort, and energy on the part of librarians all over the city searching for information about the same topics. By creating and then promoting the science Web page, students have the same starting point from their school or public library.
2. To introduce students to the concepts of The Big6™ (Eisenberg and Berkowitz, 1988). The Big6™ is an information problem solving approach created by Robert Berkowitz and Michael Eisenberg. The purpose of the Big6™ is to provide students with a model for thinking about research by following a series of six steps.

The Big6™ is used in schools, and for that reason alone should be adapted to the public library setting. Public librarians should complement the work of media specialists to teach students the "big picture" of information problem solving, not just point to a source that answers a particular question. While I've long been an advocate of a proactive role of public librarians in providing instruction, the coming of the information explosion makes the need ever more immediate. My previous work in providing instruction in the public library setting had focused on process more than product; but exposure to the Big6™ model helped me think of information instruction as another form of problem solving. As solving problems *is* the role of the public library, the Big6™ model answers our needs for instruction with the students' need for an efficient, effective, and even interesting approach to solving information problems like the science fair.

Caroline's comments presented at the start of this chapter are just one of many positive things students at the Saint Agnes Academy, a private college prep school in Houston Texas, had to say about the use of the Big6™ in their school the past two school years. For the 1996–97 school year, the school library developed four primary goals. The first was to acquaint more students with the Internet for research purposes. The second was to increase both the quantity and quality of information skills instruction. The third goal was to introduce students and faculty to the Big6™. Working more closely with teachers in planning and implementing research projects was the final goal. All four of these goals were met through one program: the development of the Big6™ project pages. These pages simply use the Big6™ steps to guide students through a process of critical thinking, skill building, and problem solving. Originally planned to coincide with only four major projects a year, this idea expanded during the 1997–98 school year with over 20 pages created. While many successful elements of this effort will be outlined in this chapter, the most important outcome has been the increased cooperation between the faculty with the library staff. In addition to providing classroom time for instruction in the library, teachers are starting to use the Big6™ to transform their research and writing assignments to make them clearer, more focused, and more student centered.

TRANSFORMING ASSIGNMENTS

At first, teachers needed to "buy in to" using the Big6™ and the Internet as viable and valuable research tools. For example, to study *The Great Gatsby* during 11th-grade English, students used the Big6™ to research topics (fads, sports, fashion, etc.) from the 1920s. When this project was first conceived years ago, it was a basic library book research project with little instruction. However, over a three-year evolution, the project became an instructional opportunity, an Internet-rich project that taught students research and critical thinking skills. After completing the research, students used the information and graphics they had found to create posters, skits, and other means to present their learning to their classmates.

The metamorphosis of *The Great Gatsby* study into a Big6™ project empowered the teachers to rethink, revise, and rewrite the assignment. It became more student centered—students researching to teach other students. It also became a critical thinking exercise—learning not just how to find information, but how to evaluate and use it. For most of the students this type of research was new. The Big6™ process provided them with an outline for thinking about, and then doing research. Most students, like Teresitte Sarmeatt, said they found the Big6™ useful because "it showed me a step-by-step process which I could use to organize myself and minimize the time it would take me to research."

Moreover, 11th graders face two other big research projects later in the term. Thus this assignment provided them with a strong foundation they could apply to those upcoming information problems.

The *Gatsby* assignment was not the only project transformed through implementation of the Big6™. Another example was the evolution of a literary analysis paper on early American romanticism. Five years ago, students merely read stories from a textbook ("Devil and Tom Walker" by Irving and "Fall of the House of Usher" by Poe). After reading the stories and discussing the authors' use of romanticism in class, students wrote a paper merely "refunding" that information. Now, students must choose their own themes from a story that is not discussed in class or found in their textbook. This allows students to utilize the skills of analysis they've been taught to develop their own ideas on theme. This process, as student Caroline Hetton commented, "made me analyze the topic more thoroughly." In addition, rather than reading from the text, students are introduced to the valuable resource of electronic text centers as they used the Internet to find primary source material. The end result has been students writing better papers about themes that intrigue them, rather than those that interest their teacher.

By simply changing the medium for the primary source material from textbook to the Internet, the assignment undergoes a transformation for many students. It is no longer just a boring paper, but rather a "cool" assignment. They learn that the Internet—that same place they chat, look at their e-mail, and search for the latest entry into the hunk-of-the-month club—also has an educational purpose. For students who are economically disadvantaged or otherwise without home access to the Internet, this type of assignment opens a new world that is new, different, and fun. And—no big surprise—it becomes more fun for the teachers. The projects that students produce are more interesting, students are more engaged, and a momentum starts building toward another Big6™ project.

By adopting the Big6™, teachers' assignments require critical thinking. Students are still given direction, but instead of assigning a topic like "how nature applied to *Jane Eyre*," students use the Big6™ to create their own topics and to plan out their research. They must choose a theme, create a thesis, and then prove it. Just as the Big6™ requires questioning ("how do I use this resource?"), assignments now put the onus for the questioning on the student's creativity rather than the teacher's ideas. The students get a framework and jumping-off point to be creative in their researching and their writing.

CREATING WEB PAGES

These Web-based project pages use the Big6™ as an outline. When students come to the library for instruction, they find one of these project pages for their research task. During instruction, we lecture about the Big6™, but also provide students with a "hands-on" walk-through using the project page covering each of the six steps. Each step asks Big6™ questions, such as "What am I supposed to do?" and then provides part of the answer via hypertext links. Eleventh-grader Wendy Vickery found this part of the process helpful because "it made me think about the questions I am supposed to ask myself." Using a standard outline assures that all of our students learn the Big6™ along with information skills, and that they do so by using the power of the Internet.

We begin each project page with the title of the research project and a short statement, normally one sentence. This statement contains a hypertext link to a specific page or, as in the *Gatsby* project, to the best category heading in *Yahoo!* regarding the research subject. Providing such a link gives students immediate access to a useful information resource and also demonstrates the Internet's value for student research.

Task Definition, the first step in the Big6™, requires teachers to provide librarians with a copy of the assignment. The assignment sheet explains the ins-and-outs of the task to be completed. For some teachers, the task definition is short, just a paragraph or two, while others provide a lengthier document, and many ask for the librarians' input on designing the research assignment. We "mark up" the document with HTML and then set it up as a separate Web page linked from the Big6™ project page.

Information Seeking Strategies is the most labor-intensive part of putting together project pages. In this part of the project page we define types of sources, identify the appropriate search tools, and suggest possible resources. In many ways, this section is nothing more than a hypertext pathfinder. It still lists reference books, but expands to list electronic resources, many which are only a click away. There is also a short list of search engines. As part of instruction on accessing information (step 3 in the Big6™), students learn the basics of searching *Yahoo!*, *AltaVista*, or *Hotbot*. Following the search engines is a list of between six and twelve appropriate Web pages to find information to complete the task. Some of these links are to specific pages, normally sites that are indexes or hotlists to the selected topic, like *Flapper Station* for the

Gatsby assignment. Others links are to the *Yahoo!* category subject heading, some to commercial information sites with search engines of their own, like *CNN* or online periodicals such as the *New York Times,* and some link to rich content sites. The sites listed are suggestions; students are not required to use them. The hope is that this part of the project page provides a "level playing field" to get everyone some basic information, and then encouraging and teaching them on how to find more on their own.

Location and Access issues are primarily answered during instruction, although there are links to pages about using search engines. This step, however, is primarily taught through hands-on work with students. In addition to teaching search engines, developing complex searches, and understanding search results, we do basic instruction on using the Netscape browser. It does no good to elaborate on the intricacies of Boolean logic and demonstrate complicated searches if students don't first know how to do simple tasks such as navigating, saving, downloading, printing, etc. This leads to other instructional opportunities, in particular for those students who want to create graphic-heavy presentations. Use of color printers, graphic converters, scanners, and—for seniors working on a similar project—basic instruction for PowerPoint are also covered as an adjunct to instruction. In doing so, seniors have seen their research projects transformed from a "check-out-books/write-a-report process" to one that develops critical thinking skills and provides them with experience using the Internet, PowerPoint, and other technologies.

Use of Information is the next step in Big6™. The main emphasis on the project pages, and in instruction, for this step is on evaluating Web resources. There is a link to a page about evaluation and it is reinforced through lecture. Students need to learn this critical thinking skill and how to determine a Web page's value to their research. Many students see the Internet as the panacea and think because it is on the Net that it is good as gold. Separating the real gold from fool's gold is an important skill for students to master. Eleventh-grader Angela Dunn noted how the Big6™, "made me think about the sources I was using and their reliability. It also helped me to narrow down all of the information until I got to just the necessities."

Synthesis includes a link to a document on citing electronic resources. In addition, students receive a handout during instruction with more detailed information. For most students, the teacher determines how the research will be presented. The teacher will then provide the students with an evaluation of this work presented in the form of a grade.

As the final step in the Big6™, we encourage students to **Evaluate their Process**. Using a simple form submission script, students answer questions about their work on the project, as well as on the effectiveness of the project page. Their comments are insightful and rewarding, such as 11th-grader Courtney Samphul who noted that the "Big6™ process taught her how to research her project quickly and efficiently. She was able to learn about the different search engines and use them without difficulty. Similarly, Kate Krayauk commented that the Big6™, "helped me organize my self, my thoughts, and my information." By taking time to examine the process, students should begin to see areas for improvement in solving information problems. Helping students improve their ability to solve information problems is why we built these Big6™ project pages. We want to see our students working efficiently, effectively, and always improving. We want them to work smarter, not harder, on every project. We want all students to be able to say, as 11th-grader Natalia Lentino did, that they were "able to make connections from what I had learned from the Big6™ and facilitate the research of the next assignment paper."

Faculty have responded enthusiastically to these Big6™ pages and are advocates of the process. Margaret Buehler said, after the *Gatsby* project, that:

> As an English teacher, I tended to be stuck between the covers of books; they were my comfort zone. Since the introduction of Big6™ pages, I have been able to incorporate books and Internet into exciting lessons and projects which have offered my students real data and the opportunity to do their own research. The kids have become much more adept both with technical use of the Net and with sifting through the information to find what is valuable and reliable.

And they had fun doing it. Students enjoyed using a digital camera to take pictures of themselves in 1920s' garb for their presentation and posting them on the Web page. Small things, such as using icons, photos, and the like give the pages a more appealing, highly graphical look. Again, the Big6™ allows librarians, teachers, and students to move from textbook assignments to ones that are student centered, fun, and teach critical thinking and other critically important skills.

EVERYBODY WINS

These project pages present "win-win-win" situations. Students "win" as they get a framework, practical and philosophical, to complete research. On their evaluations, they include comments, such as one made by 11th-grader Maureen Leang-Kee that "it helped me understand what types of sources I needed and how or where to find them." Teachers "win" as they find students doing better research. Margaret Buehler discovered after the first assignment that she now has a much closer working relationship with the library and librarians, as do her students. In addition, the use of the Big6™ method has made her write better assignments; and her students understand what to do, how to approach the task, and what the criteria for evaluation will be before they begin the assignment. Thus, their finished product is of much higher quality than she expected.

Finally, the library "wins" as these Big6™ project pages have allowed the library to illustrate the importance of instruction, information skills, and the Internet. In doing so, the library serves students better, works more closely with faculty, and demonstrates the significance of the library media center to the school. Visit the library's home page (*www.st-agnes.org/library*) to view the *Gatsby* project page and others.

REFERENCE

Michael Eisenberg, and Robert Berkowitz. 1988. *Information Problem Solving: The Big Six Skills Approach to Library & Information Skills Instruction*. Norwood, NJ: Abex Publishing.

Chapter 12

YA Customer Service Matters!

Patrick Jones

It is essential that all of us who work in libraries create caring environments that serve young adult customers well because of one fact: Kids who read succeed.

It is really that simple.

Research is a funny thing. One study proves one thing; another proves exactly the opposite. Is it healthy to eat shrimp? Is coffee good or bad for you? Will you live longer if you do drink a little wine or if you don't? Who knows? What works? What doesn't?

But educational research is clear on one point: Kids who read succeed. It is more than a slogan. It is fact. Stephen Krashen's book *The Power of Reading*—what a wonderful title!—looks at years and years of reading studies (1993). Guess what? Kids who read succeed. But what makes a reader?

There it gets a little trickier. But the research supports three causal elements:

1. access to reading materials (notice I didn't say books);
2. access to good role models; and
3. personal satisfaction. That is, readers read because it brings them satisfaction ("Adolescent Literacy Comes of Age," 1999).

Access to reading materials is critical. Sometimes you hear that "teens don't read anymore." Well that is true, and it also is not true. Few people read as many books today as they might have in preceding generations. It is not just the influence of TV. It is the influence of TV and cable TV and radio and computers and video games and scores of other choices that were not available previously. It is the influence of affluence. It is the influence of choices. Since when did choices become a bad thing?

I believe that teens are reading as much as ever, they are just reading "different." They are wired different. Most teens can read a book and listen to the radio while also carrying on real or virtual conversations. Teens multi-task media. And they also read different formats. Few generations of teens have even read YA literature, as its modern era dates only from the late sixties. Just within the last decade, dire predictions of the death of the YA novel were being written. Today the form is enjoying a true renaissance with exciting new authors demonstrating grit and girth of vision in beautifully written and powerful books that speak directly to the hearts and minds of young adults (Aronson, 1997; Cart, 1997; Cooper and Zvirin, 1998; November, 1997; and Rosen, 1997). While YA literature is *not* the center of the world for most teens, it is getting better.

And the marketplace is huge. Just as the world has changed from every teen listening to the same Top 40 tunes to the current, shrapnel-like explosion of forty different musical genres, the YA book is more than a problem novel, a series romance, horror or mystery, or science fiction or fantasy. It is a literature of diverse genres that reflects, in one way or another, one "super-genre"—the coming of age story that asks (and usually answers) the question, "Am I the only one?"

So kids do read books. But that is not all. Just about every study of teen reading interests concludes that books are not the primary reading material of most teens, magazines are. Again, the marketplace is alive. Stalwarts like *Teen* and *Sports Illustrated* have been joined by a host of new titles. The world of YA magazines is on fire, and with good reason. Becoming a teenager is all about developing special interests; magazines have always been aimed at peoples' special interests. So, as the interest of YAs in the world has grown, publishers have recognized the opportunity to expand the scope of the reading material available.

But kids read other things—computer screens, for example. And they write. Would any one like to argue whether or not teens are writing more now in their "recreational time" than ever before? No, it's true that chat room conversations, e-mail messages, bulletin board postings, and real-time online gaming talk is not always formal, grammatically correct English. Instead the writing is short and to the point. It is conversation in a written format. But it is writing and it is reading. We have evolved beyond the stereotype of the teenager with the phone glued to his/her head to that of the teenager reading and writing and chatting and e-mailing and posting on the computer that never seems to be turned off.

So, the key to providing teens with the means to accomplish their developmentally important language activities turns out to be access. Access is what libraries do. The world of information is one set and the world of teenagers is the other. The library is the point where those worlds can and do and should and must connect. By selecting, organizing, and distributing information, libraries provide access. From simple things like a library card to things as complex and expensive as the design, construction, and maintenance of wide area networks, libraries are about access. From chaining the books to the shelves in ancient times to unchaining the power and the glory of the Internet to youth today, libraries provide access to reading materials. We have come full circle; the magic circle of reading.

Reading provides teens with assets. The words provide them with support, the ideas empower them, it is a constructive use of their time, it solidifies their own commitment to learning, it teaches—well, not all reading but lots of it—positive values. We must give them opportunities to think, talk, and write about their reading—shouldn't every library have a *Harry Potter* book discussion group?—to improve their academic skills, their social skills, and finally to help provide them with a positive identity. The elements of that identity—personal power, self-esteem, sense of purpose, and positive view of a personal future—are the elements of young adult literature and can be important facets of young adult library service as well.

Kids who read succeed. Libraries that support teen readers succeed. Kids and libraries that succeed will create communities that succeed. Communities that succeed build development assets for youth. Youth who build assets become readers. Kids who read succeed. It is a Mobius strip. Not a mystery, but a Mobius strip of success. A magic circle that connects young adults and libraries.

On the most basic level, what kids need and what libraries offer is an opportunity to develop relationships. Every reference question, every customer service interaction is an example of a fleeting (and in some cases, perhaps, not so fleeting) relationship. How we treat that teen in that moment, during that moment of truth, means so much.

Listed below are your six keys to asset building. At the reference desk, the circulation desk, during an outreach activity, and especially in your everyday life, you can build the assets you need to work effectively with young adults.

1. Everyone counts: The YA librarian is not the only asset builder, everyone counts. Everyone contributes. A smile builds assets.
2. Treat every teen as an asset: Not just those kids the media have stereotyped as at-risk; every teen is at risk of not having enough assets. Take no teen for granted.
3. Asset building is ongoing: Know that the child you helped find the picture book should come back in ten years to seek out financial aid information. Aim for the ongoing relationship.

4. Consistent message: Start a trend today of thanking every teen who comes into the library. Do it over and over until it becomes common for everyone on the staff to say. But you start it.

5. Redundancy: Don't get tired of saying it. Marketing research tells us how everyone needs to hear the same message over and over (awareness) before they believe it or do something with it (action). Every day you can create the awareness that we want teens in libraries.

6. Relationships are the key: From the telephone reference interview, to the booktalk, to breaking up a fight, we need to get to know kids. Learn their names, tell them yours. Simply let them know that you care. Relationships are the key to demolishing stereotypes, improving services, and building assets.

Libraries are not passive repositories of books anymore, if they ever were. And librarians today do not fit the negative stereotypes of the past. As libraries have evolved into modern, dynamic, responsive institutions, librarians have become proactive, positive, and powerful agents of change. Yes, there is power in the political system that establishes the budget, in the director's or principal's office to set priorities, but the greatest power remains in those one-on-one encounters, those relationships we have with teens. Teens are not problems to be solved, they are customers to be served allowing all of us to "win" during the moment of truth.

REFERENCES

"Adolescent Literacy Comes of Age." 1999. *Reading Teacher* (August): 22.

Aronson, Marc. 1997. "The Challenge and the Glory of Young Adult Literature." *Booklist* (April 15): 1418–1419.

Cart, Michael. 1997. "Not Just for Children Anymore." *Booklist* (November 15): 553.

Cooper, Ilene, and Stephanie Zvirin. 1998. "Publishing on the Edge." *Booklist* (January 1–15): 792:3.

Krashen, Stephen. 1993. *The Power of Reading*. Englewood, CO: Libraries Unlimited.

November, Sharyn. 1997. "We're Not 'Young Adults'—We're Prisoners of Life." *Voice of Youth Advocates* (August): 169–172.

Rosen, Judith. 1997. "Breaking the Age Barrier." *Publishers Weekly* (September 8): 28–31.

Index

About the Authors

PATRICK JONES

Patrick Jones runs *Connectingya.com* a firm dedicated to consulting, training, and coaching for providing powerful youth services. Jones was the Youth Services Coordinator for the Houston Public Library in Houston, Texas when it planned, developed, and implemented the award-winning *Power Card Challenge* program to register every child for a library card, and the *ASPIRE* after-school program for at-risk middle school kids which was named as one of the top five programs in the nation serving young adults by the Young Adult Library Services Association (YALSA). He is the author of *Connecting Young Adults and Libraries: A How To Do It Manual* (Neal-Schuman, 1992). A second revised and expanded edition was published in 1998. Jones also published in 1998 the first volume in the Scarecrow Press Young Adult series called *What's So Scary About R.L. Stine?* In addition, Jones has written over 50 articles for such library professional publications as *The Horn Book, School Library Journal, Voice of Youth Advocates, Public Libraries, American Libraries,* and *The Journal of Popular Culture in Libraries,* as well as essays for reference books such as *Children's Books and Their Creators* (Houghton Mifflin, 1995) and the *Saint James Encyclopedia of Popular Culture* (Gale Research, 2000). He is a frequent speaker at library conferences across the United States, as well as in Canada, Australia, and New Zealand. He created the web pages *Young Adult Librarian's Help/Homepage* and *Virtual YA: A Directory of Public Library YA Web pages.* He is a former member of the Board of Directors of YALSA, as well as serving on the association's Quick Picks, Teen Hoopla, and Publications committees. He currently serves on the professional development committee. Jones won the VOYA/Frances Henne Research Award from YALSA for research on customer service to young adults in urban public libraries. He has just finished his first young adult novel (*Things Change*) and is working on a professional book about library card campaigns and a revision of YALSA's *Directions for Library Services to Young Adults.*

JOEL SHOEMAKER

Joel Shoemaker is the library media specialist at South East Junior High in Iowa City, IA, where he lives with his wife, Becky, and their two sons. Joel's professional preparation includes a bachelor's degree in English Education (1972) and Master's in Education (1975) specializing in the teaching of reading from the University of Illinois, Urbana, and a Master of Arts (Library Science, 1989) from the University of Northern Iowa, Cedar Falls, IA. His nearly thirty years of teaching experience have been primarily with middle-school and junior-high aged teens. He has also taught as an Adjunct Instructor for the School of Library and Information Science, University of Iowa, Iowa City, IA, for several years, conducted numerous successful and popular workshops and other classes about young adult literature, and has been recognized for his advocacy for teens and improved young adult library services. He served as a judge for the Society of Childrens' Book Writers "Golden Kite Award" in 1991, was a member of the Young Adult Library Services Association (YALSA) Best Books for Young Adults Committee 1991–93; chaired that committee in 1993–94; was a member of the YALSA Board of Directors 1994–97; served as YALSA President-Elect, President, and Past President 1998–2000. He is also a member of the American Association of School Librarians, the National Education Association, and other professional organizations, including the Iowa Educational Media Association for which he has served as a member of the Board of Directors and currently is co-chair of the Iowa Teen Award. He is currently chair of the panel of judges for the Los Angeles Times Young Adult Fiction Award. Joel has been a long-time reviewer for *School Library Journal* and other professional journals where he has also published several articles. Published annually in *VOYA (The Voice of Youth Advocates)* since June, 1997, his interviews with young adult authors have included Rob Thomas, Will Hobbs, Michael Cadnum, Randy Powell, and Todd Strasser. *Skateboarding Streetstyle* (Capstone, 1995) was his first book.